Gheo-Shih

Prehistory and Human Ecology of the Valley of Oaxaca

Kent V. Flannery and Joyce Marcus, General Editors

Volume 1 *The Use of Land and Water Resources in the Past and Present Valley of Oaxaca, Mexico*, by Anne V.T. Kirkby. Memoirs of the Museum of Anthropology, University of Michigan, No. 5. 1973.

Volume 2 *Sociopolitical Aspects of Canal Irrigation in the Valley of Oaxaca*, by Susan H. Lees. Memoirs of the Museum of Anthropology, University of Michigan, No. 6. 1973.

Volume 3 *Formative Mesoamerican Exchange Networks with Special Reference to the Valley of Oaxaca*, by Jane W. Pires-Ferreira. Memoirs of the Museum of Anthropology, University of Michigan, No. 7. 1975.

Volume 4 *Fábrica San José and Middle Formative Society in the Valley of Oaxaca*, by Robert D. Drennan. Memoirs of the Museum of Anthropology, University of Michigan, No. 8. 1976.

Volume 5 Part 1. *The Vegetational History of the Oaxaca Valley*, by C. Earle Smith, Jr. Part 2. *Zapotec Plant Knowledge: Classification, Uses and Communication*, by Ellen Messer. Memoirs of the Museum of Anthropology, University of Michigan, No. 10. 1978.

Volume 6 *Excavations at Santo Domingo Tomaltepec: Evolution of a Formative Community in the Valley of Oaxaca, Mexico*, by Michael E. Whalen. Memoirs of the Museum of Anthropology, University of Michigan, No. 12. 1981.

Volume 7 *Monte Albán's Hinterland, Part 1: The Prehispanic Settlement Patterns of the Central and Southern Parts of the Valley of Oaxaca, Mexico*, by Richard E. Blanton, Stephen Kowalewski, Gary Feinman, and Jill Appel. Memoirs of the Museum of Anthropology, University of Michigan, No. 15. 1982.

Volume 8 *Chipped Stone Tools in Formative Oaxaca, Mexico: Their Procurement, Production and Use*, by William J. Parry. Memoirs of the Museum of Anthropology, University of Michigan, No. 20. 1987.

Volume 9 *Agricultural Intensification and Prehistoric Health in the Valley of Oaxaca, Mexico*, by Denise C. Hodges. Memoirs of the Museum of Anthropology, University of Michigan, No. 22. 1989.

Volume 10 *Early Formative Pottery of the Valley of Oaxaca*, by Kent V. Flannery and Joyce Marcus, with ceramic analysis by William O. Payne. Memoirs of the Museum of Anthropology, University of Michigan, No. 27. 1994.

Volume 11 *Women's Ritual in Formative Oaxaca: Figurine-Making, Divination, Death and the Ancestors*, by Joyce Marcus. Memoirs of the Museum of Anthropology, University of Michigan, No. 33. 1998.

Volume 12 *The Sola Valley and the Monte Albán State: A Study of Zapotec Imperial Expansion*, by Andrew K. Balkansky. Memoirs of the Museum of Anthropology, University of Michigan, No. 36. 2002.

Volume 13 *Excavations at San José Mogote 1: The Household Archaeology*, by Kent V. Flannery and Joyce Marcus. Memoirs of the Museum of Anthropology, University of Michigan, No. 40. 2005.

Volume 14 *Excavations at Cerro Tilcajete: A Monte Albán II Administrative Center in the Valley of Oaxaca*, by Christina Elson. Memoirs of the Museum of Anthropology, University of Michigan, No. 42. 2007.

Volume 15 *Cerro Danush: Excavations at a Hilltop Community in the Eastern Valley of Oaxaca, Mexico*, by Ronald K. Faulseit. Memoirs of the Museum of Anthropology, University of Michigan, No. 54. 2013.

Volume 16 *Excavations at San José Mogote 2: The Cognitive Archaeology*, by Kent V. Flannery and Joyce Marcus. Memoirs of the Museum of Anthropology, University of Michigan, No. 58. 2015.

Volume 17 *Cueva Blanca: Social Change in the Archaic of the Valley of Oaxaca*, by Kent V. Flannery and Frank Hole. Memoirs of the Museum of Anthropology, University of Michigan, No. 60. 2019.

Volume 18 *Zapotec Monuments and Political History*, by Joyce Marcus. Memoirs of the Museum of Anthropology, University of Michigan, No. 61. 2020.

Volume 19 *Gheo-Shih: An Archaic Macroband Camp in the Valley of Oaxaca*, by Frank Hole and Kent V. Flannery. Memoirs of the Museum of Anthropology, University of Michigan, No. 66. 2024.

Related Volumes

Flannery, Kent V.
  2009 *Guilá Naquitz: Archaic Foraging and Early Agriculture in Oaxaca, Mexico*. Walnut Creek, CA: Left Coast Press.

Flannery, Kent V., and Joyce Marcus
  2003 *The Cloud People: Divergent Evolution of the Zapotec and Mixtec Civilizations*. Clinton Corners, New York: Percheron Press.

Marcus, Joyce, and Kent V. Flannery
  1996 *Zapotec Civilization: How Urban Society Evolved in Mexico's Oaxaca Valley*. London: Thames and Hudson.

A sample of Jícaras phase projectile points from Gheo-Shih.

Memoirs of the Museum of Anthropology
University of Michigan
Number 66

PREHISTORY AND HUMAN ECOLOGY OF THE VALLEY OF OAXACA
Kent V. Flannery and Joyce Marcus, General Editors
Volume 19

Gheo-Shih
An Archaic Macroband Camp in the Valley of Oaxaca

Frank Hole and Kent V. Flannery

Ann Arbor, Michigan
2024

©2024 by the Regents of the University of Michigan
The Museum of Anthropology
All rights reserved

Printed in the United States of America
ISBN (print) 978-1-951538-77-4
ISBN (ebook) 978-1-951538-78-1

Cover design by Bruce Worden

The University of Michigan Museum of Anthropological Archaeology (UMMAA) Press publishes books on archaeology and anthropology.

Browse/buy this and all UMMAA Press books at **sites.lsa.umich.edu/archaeology-books**
Visit the Museum's website at **lsa.umich.edu/ummaa**
View this book on Fulcrum.org at **https://doi.org/10.3998/mpub.14477325**

For permissions, questions, or manuscript queries, contact Museum publications in Ann Arbor, Michigan, by email at umma-pubs@umich.edu.

Library of Congress Control Number: 2024934731

The paper used in this publication meets the requirements of the ANSI Standard Z39.48-1984 (Permanence of Paper).

Table of Contents

List of Illustrations	ix
List of Tables	xiv
Acknowledgments	xv

Part I. Introduction

Chapter 1: The Discovery of Gheo-Shih	3
Chapter 2: The Systematic Surface Pickup	10
Chapter 3: Systematic Testing and the Establishment of Areas A and C	16
Chapter 4: A Naquitz Phase Ritual Feature in Area A	33

Part II. The Jícaras Phase Artifacts

Chapter 5: Chipped Stone Tools: The Typology	41
Chapter 6: Chipped Stone Tools: The Horizontal Distribution	75
Chapter 7: Projectile Points: The Typology	100
Chapter 8: Projectile Points: The Horizontal Distribution	113
Chapter 9: Ground Stone Tools	116
Chapter 10: Ornaments	122

Part III. Ancillary Studies

Chapter 11: Pollen Samples	129
Chapter 12: Radiocarbon Dates	132

Part IV. Summary and Conclusions

Chapter 13: Gheo-Shih vs. Guilá Naquitz: The Differences between Microband and Macroband Camps	137
Chapter 14: Gheo-Shih's Place in the Oaxaca Archaic	141

Appendix A: Resumen en Español, by Jhon Cruz Quiñones	145
References	147

List of Illustrations

Frontispiece: A sample of Jícaras phase projectile points from Gheo-Shih.

1.1. Map of the eastern Valley of Oaxaca, *4*
1.2. Photograph of the site of Gheo-Shih, seen from the cliffs to the west, *5*
1.3. The lands of the ex-hacienda El Fuerte, showing Archaic sites, watercourses, and elevations in meters, *6*
1.4. Four vegetation zones and eight facies of vegetation on the lands of the ex-hacienda El Fuerte, *7*
1.5. The mesquite facies of Mesquite Grassland B, near the Río Mitla, showing the so-called Mitla Fortress, *9*

2.1. Photograph of a crew of 12 searching for artifacts on the southern part of the Gheo-Shih site, *11*
2.2. The grid of 5 x 5 m squares used for the systematic surface pickup at Gheo-Shih, *12*
2.3. Photograph of Gheo-Shih from the cliffs to the northwest, *13*
2.4. A copper bell of the Monte Albán V period, *13*
2.5. The distribution of projectile points, or fragments thereof, recovered from the surface of Gheo-Shih, *14*
2.6. Diagram showing the 5 x 5 m square used for surface survey divided into twenty-five 1 x 1 m squares for the purpose of testing and excavation, *15*

3.1. Excavating the test pits that led to the creation of Area A, *17*
3.2. The crew lays out a series of test pits in Area A, *18*
3.3. Looking northeast over Area A during the course of excavation, *19*
3.4. Grid of 1 x 1 m squares established for Area A at Gheo-Shih, *20*
3.5. A workman in Area A cross-sections a soil discoloration to determine whether or not it is a posthole, *21*
3.6. A soil discoloration that turned out to be a rodent burrow, *21*
3.7. A Pedernales point, found in situ in square H25/a5 of Area A's Jícaras phase component, *22*
3.8. Workmen testing Area B of Gheo-Shih, *23*
3.9. Grid of 1 x 1 m squares established for Area C of Gheo-Shih; all were excavated, *23*
3.10. The excavation of the lower component (b) of Area C by alternate 1 x 1 m squares, *24*
3.11. A Pedernales point, found in situ in square E15/e1 of Area C's lower component (b), *25*
3.12. The grid of 1 x 1 m squares used for the lower component (b) of Area C, *26*
3.13. The excavation grid for Area C, showing the location of the five best defined hearths or roasting pits found in the upper component (a), *26*
3.14. The remains of a rock-lined hearth or roasting pit in square D14/e3, Area C, *27*
3.15. The remains of a rock-lined hearth or roasting pit in square E15/a4, Area C, *28*
3.16. A view of the southern part of Area C during excavation, *28*
3.17. Grid of lower component (b) of Area C, characterized by occasional lenses of gravel at varying depths, *29*
3.18. Two workmen remove a gravel lens in Area C, component (b), *31*
3.19. The location of Areas A and C within the grid created for the systematic surface pickup of Gheo-Shih, *32*

4.1. Photograph of the basal level of Area A, seen from the northwest corner of the excavation, *34*
4.2. A plan drawing of the basal level of Area A, *35*
4.3. Photograph of Feature 1, seen from the south, *36*
4.4. Photograph of the basal level of Area A, seen from the north (Square G25), *37*

5.1. A hammerstone from the Jícaras phase component of Area A, *42*
5.2. A hammerstone from the lower component (b) of Area C, *42*
5.3. A hammerstone from the upper component (a) of Area C, *43*
5.4. Two hammerstones from the Jícaras phase component of Area A, *43*
5.5. Two flake cores from the Jícaras phase component of Area A, *44*
5.6. Two flake cores from the Jícaras phase component of Area A, *44*
5.7. A flake core from the Jícaras phase component of Area A, *45*
5.8. A flake core from the lower component (b) of Area C, *45*
5.9. A small flake core from Test Pit G21/e5, *46*
5.10. Four fragments of flake cores from Gheo-Shih, *47*
5.11. Utilized flakes from the upper component (a) of Area C, *47*
5.12. Two utilized flakes from Area C, *48*
5.13. Three notched flakes from Area C, *48*
5.14. Four notched flakes from the lower component (b) of Area C, *49*
5.15. A notched flake from the surface (Square C13), *49*
5.16. A flake with bulbar end retouch from the lower component (b) of Area C, *49*
5.17. Two flakes with bulbar end retouch from the lower component (b) of Area C, *49*
5.18. A crude blade from the Jícaras phase component of Area A, *50*
5.19. Three blades from the Jícaras phase component of Area A, *50*
5.20. A blade from the lower component (b) of Area C, *50*
5.21. A blade with retouch from the lower component (b) of Area C, *50*
5.22. Two blades with retouch from the lower component (b) of Area C, *51*
5.23. A segment of retouched blade from the lower component (b) of Area C, *51*
5.24. Two blades with retouch from Gheo-Shih, *51*
5.25. A flake with sheen from the lower component (b) of Area C, *52*
5.26. A flake with sheen from the Jícaras phase component of Area A, *52*
5.27. Two flakes with sheen from the lower component (b) of Area C, *52*
5.28. A sickle from the lower component (b) of Area C, *53*
5.29. A fragment of sickle from the Jícaras phase component of Area A, *53*
5.30. A fragment of sickle from the lower component (b) of Area C, *53*
5.31. A chopper made from a cobble, found in Test Pit E22/e1, *54*
5.32. A large end scraper from the Jícaras phase component of Area A, *55*
5.33. Two small end scrapers from the Jícaras phase component of Area A, *55*
5.34. A large end scraper from the lower component (b) of Area C, *55*
5.35. A large end scraper from the lower component (b) of Area C, *55*
5.36. Two small end scrapers from the lower component (b) of Area C, *56*
5.37. An end scraper from the surface (Square H3), *56*
5.38. A small end scraper from the surface (Square L11), *56*
5.39. An end scraper from the surface (Square F10), *56*
5.40. Two sidescrapers/knives from the lower component (b) of Area C, *57*
5.41. Two sidescrapers/knives from the lower component (b) of Area C, *57*
5.42. A sidescraper/knife from the surface (Square D29), *57*
5.43. A sidescraper/knife from the surface (Square C24), *58*
5.44. A sidescraper/knife from the surface (Square I11), *58*
5.45. A steep denticulate scraper from the Jícaras phase component of Area A, *58*
5.46. Two steep denticulate scrapers from the Jícaras phase component of Area A, *58*
5.47. Two steep denticulate scrapers from the lower component (b) of Area C, *59*
5.48. Two steep denticulate scrapers from the lower component (b) of Area C, *59*
5.49. A steep denticulate scraper from the boundary between the upper and lower components of Area C, *60*

5.50. A fragment of steep denticulate scraper from the upper component (a) of Area C, *60*
5.51. Two burins from the upper component (a) of Area C, *61*
5.52. A burin from the lower component (b) of Area C, *61*
5.53. Two burins from the lower component (b) of Area C, *61*
5.54. A burin from the surface (Square I14), *61*
5.55. A burin from the surface (Square S5), *61*
5.56. A burin from the surface (Square BB27), *61*
5.57. A burin from the surface (Square P2), *62*
5.58. A burin from the surface (Square F19), *62*
5.59. A burin from the surface (Square H14), *62*
5.60. A burin from the surface (Square H15), *62*
5.61. A burin from the surface (Square C18), *62*
5.62. A burin from the surface (Square I24), *63*
5.63. Large drills (or fragments thereof) from Gheo-Shih, *63*
5.64. A large drill from the Jícaras phase component of Area A, *64*
5.65. A small drill/perforator from the Jícaras phase component of Area A, *64*
5.66. A small drill/perforator from the lower component (b) of Area C, *64*
5.67. A small drill/perforator from the upper component (a) of Area C, *64*
5.68. A damaged Variety A biface from the surface of Gheo-Shih, *65*
5.69. A broken Variety A biface from the surface, *65*
5.70. A broken Variety A biface from the surface, *66*
5.71. The tapered ends of two Variety A bifaces from the surface, *67*
5.72. The tapered end of a Variety A biface, found on the surface in Square I8, *68*
5.73. A damaged Variety A biface from the surface, *68*
5.74. A damaged Variety A biface from the upper component (a) of Area C, *68*
5.75. Four fragments of Variety A bifaces, recovered from the surface of Gheo-Shih, *69*
5.76. A damaged Variety B biface, found on the surface some 100 m south of the site of Gheo-Shih, *69*
5.77. The base of a broken Variety B biface, found on the surface of Gheo-Shih (Square K30), *70*
5.78. A damaged Variety B biface recovered from the surface (Square L30), *70*
5.79. Two fragments of Variety B bifaces recovered from the surface of Gheo-Shih, *70*
5.80. Two fragments of Variety B bifaces from the upper component (a) of Area C, *71*
5.81. A broken Variety B biface from the lower component (b) of Area C, *71*
5.82. A small Variety C biface from the Jícaras phase component of Area A, *71*
5.83. A broken Variety C biface from the Jícaras phase component of Area A, *71*
5.84. Variety C bifaces from the Jícaras phase component of Area A, *72*
5.85. A Variety C biface from the upper component (a) of Area C, *72*
5.86. A damaged Variety C biface from the lower component (b) of Area C, *73*
5.87. A damaged Variety C biface from the lower component (b) of Area C, *73*
5.88. A small Variety C biface from the upper component (a) of Area C, *73*
5.89. A broken Variety C biface from the surface of Gheo-Shih (Square BB30), *74*
5.90. Two fragments of Variety C bifaces recovered from the surface, *74*

6.1. The distribution of hammerstones throughout the Jícaras phase component of Area A, *77*
6.2. The distribution of flake cores throughout the Jícaras phase component of Area A, *78*
6.3. The distribution of debitage throughout the Jícaras phase component of Area A, *79*
6.4. The distribution of utilized flakes throughout the Jícaras phase component of Area A, *80*
6.5. The distribution of notched flakes throughout the Jícaras phase component of Area A, *81*
6.6. The distribution of crude blades (plain) throughout the Jícaras phase component of Area A, *83*

6.7. The distribution of end scrapers throughout the Jícaras phase component of Area A, *84*
6.8. The distribution of sidescrapers/knives throughout the Jícaras phase component of Area A, *85*
6.9. The distribution of steep denticulate scrapers throughout the Jícaras phase component of Area A, *86*
6.10. The distribution of burins throughout the Jícaras phase component of Area A, *87*
6.11. The distribution of drills throughout the Jícaras phase-component of Area A, *88*
6.12. The distribution of Variety B bifaces throughout the Jícaras phase component of Area A, *89*
6.13. The distribution of Variety C bifaces throughout the Jícaras phase component of Area A, *90*
6.14. The distribution of hammerstones throughout the lower component (b) of Area C, *92*
6.15. The distribution of flake cores throughout the lower component (b) of Area C, *92*
6.16. The distribution of debitage throughout the lower component (b) of Area C, by 1 x 1 m square, *92*
6.17. The distribution of utilized flakes throughout the lower component (b) of Area C, *92*
6.18. The distribution of notched flakes throughout the lower component (b) of Area C, *93*
6.19. The distribution of flakes with bulbar end retouch throughout the lower component (b) of Area C, *93*
6.20. The distribution of crude blades (plain) throughout the lower component (b) of Area C, *93*
6.21. The distribution of crude blades (retouched) throughout the lower component (b) of Area C, *93*
6.22. The distribution of end scrapers throughout the lower component (b) of Area C, *94*
6.23. The distribution of sidescrapers/knives throughout the lower component (b) of Area C, *94*
6.24. The distribution of steep denticulate scrapers throughout the lower component (b) of Area C, *94*
6.25. The distribution of burins throughout the lower component (b) of Area C, *94*
6.26. The distribution of drills throughout the lower component (b) of Area C, *95*
6.27. The distribution of Variety A bifaces throughout the lower component (b) of Area C, *95*
6.28. The distribution of Variety B bifaces throughout the lower component (b) of Area C, *95*
6.29. The distribution of Variety C bifaces throughout the lower component (b) of Area C, *95*
6.30. The distribution of hammerstones throughout the upper component (a) of Area C, *97*
6.31. The distribution of flake cores throughout the upper component (a) of Area C, *97*
6.32. The distribution of debitage throughout the upper component (a) of Area C, by 1 x 1 m square, *97*
6.33. The distribution of utilized flakes throughout the upper component (a) of Area C, *97*
6.34. The distribution of notched flakes throughout the upper component (a) of Area C, *98*
6.35. The distribution of crude blades (plain) throughout the upper component (a) of Area C, *98*
6.36. The distribution of sidescrapers/knives throughout the upper component (a) of Area C, *98*
6.37. The distribution of steep denticulate scrapers throughout the upper component (a) of Area C, *98*
6.38. The distribution of burins throughout the upper component (a) of Area C, *99*

7.1. A complete Pedernales point found on the surface near Guilá Naquitz Cave, *101*
7.2. Slightly damaged Pedernales point from the lower component (b) of Area C, *101*
7.3. Repaired Pedernales point from the surface of Gheo-Shih, *102*
7.4. Damaged Pedernales point recovered from the surface of Gheo-Shih after the initial excavation, *102*
7.5. Two damaged Pedernales points from the surface of Gheo-Shih, *102*
7.6. Photographs of the same two Pedernales points shown in Figure 7.5, *103*
7.7. Reworked Pedernales points, found on the dirt road just north of Gheo-Shih, *103*
7.8. Extensively reworked Pedernales point from the surface of Gheo-Shih (Square L23), *103*
7.9. Damaged Pedernales point from the Jícaras phase component of Area A, *104*
7.10. Heavily reworked Pedernales point from the Jícaras phase component of Area, *104*
7.11. Damaged Pedernales point from the surface of Gheo-Shih (Square H26), *104*
7.12. Two damaged Pedernales points from the surface of Gheo-Shih, *105*
7.13. Two damaged Pedernales points from the surface of Gheo-Shih, *105*
7.14. Stems from broken Pedernales points, recovered from the surface of Gheo-Shih, *105*
7.15. Two Trinidad points from the surface of Gheo-Shih, *106*

7.16. Photographs of the same two Trinidad points shown in Figure 7.15, *106*
7.17. Two San Nicolás points from the surface of Gheo-Shih, *107*
7.18. Photographs of the same two San Nicolás points shown in Figure 7.17, *107*
7.19. Badly broken Palmillas point from the lower component (b) of Area C, *107*
7.20. Hidalgo point from the lower component (b) of Area C, *108*
7.21. Photograph of the same Hidalgo point shown in Figure 7.20, *108*
7.22. Abasolo point from the upper component (a) of Area C, *108*
7.23. Photograph of the same Abasolo point shown in Figure 7.22, *108*
7.24. Projectile points from the Jícaras phase component of Area A; all are Pedernales points or fragments thereof, *109*
7.25. Six projectile points from the lower component (b) of Area C, *109*
7.26. Projectile points from the upper component (a) of Area C, *110*
7.27. Unclassified, badly broken point from the surface of Gheo-Shih (Square B18), *110*
7.28. The proximal half of an unclassified, badly broken point from the surface (Square S6), 110
7.29. Unclassified, badly broken point from the surface (Square F5), *110*
7.30. The proximal half of an unclassified, badly weathered point from the surface (Square B32), *110*
7.31. Unclassified, badly broken point from the surface (Square J1), 111
7.32. Four unclassified projectile point fragments from the surface of Gheo-Shih, 111
7.33. Distal end of a projectile point from the surface (Square R9), 111
7.34. Six projectile point fragments from the surface of Gheo-Shih, 112

8.1. The distribution of projectile points throughout the Jícaras phase component of Area A, 114
8.2. The distribution of projectile points throughout the lower component (b) of Area C, 115
8.3. The distribution of projectile points throughout the upper component (a) of Area C, 115

9.1. The distribution of manos and mano fragments throughout the Jícaras phase component of Area A, 117
9.2. The distribution of metate fragments throughout the Jícaras phase component of Area A, 118
9.3. The distribution of unclassified ground stone fragments throughout the Jícaras phase component of Area A, 119
9.4. The proveniences of a possible pestle (P) and stone bowl fragment (B) in the Jícaras phase component of Area A, 120
9.5. The distribution of manos and mano fragments throughout the lower component (b) of Area C, 121
9.6. The distribution of manos and mano fragments throughout the upper component (a) of Area C, 121

10.1. Two oval stone pendants recovered from the Jícaras phase component of Area A, 123
10.2. The distribution of oval pendants throughout the Jícaras phase component of Area A, 124
10.3. A fragment of biconically drilled disc recovered from the surface of Gheo-Shih (Square C9), 124
10.4. Two biconically drilled stone discs recovered from the lower component (b) of Area C, 125
10.5. Two biconically drilled stone discs from the lower component (b) of Area C, both of which broke along the centerline, 126
10.6. The distribution of biconically drilled stone discs throughout the lower component (b) of Area C, 126
10.7. Photograph and drawing of a small biconically drilled stone disc from the upper component (a) of Area C, 126
10.8. The location of the only biconically drilled stone disc recovered from the upper component (a) of Area C, 126

11.1. Five primitive maize cobs (or fragments thereof) found in ash lenses above Zone B1 at Guilá Naquitz, 131

List of Tables

6.1. Chipped stone tools from Jícaras phase levels in Area A, *76*
6.2. Chipped stone tools from the lower component (b) of Area C, *82*
6.3. Chipped stone tools from the upper component (a) of Area C, *96*

13.1. A comparison of tool frequencies at Gheo-Shih and Guilá Naquitz, *139*

Acknowledgments

The excavation of Gheo-Shih was supported by National Science Foundation Grant GS-1616. Additional funding for the analysis of artifacts was provided by Rice University and the University of Michigan.

During his excavation, Hole was assisted by Suzanne Kitchen, Barbara Hole, Marcus Winter, Richard J. Orlandini, and several other members of the Oaxaca project. Geomorphologist Michael J. Kirkby, palynologist James Schoenwetter, and botanist C. Earle Smith, Jr. routinely visited the site and provided us with crucial insights. The excavation was carried out by a team of Zapotec workmen from Mitla, whose previous experience had included the excavation of Guilá Naquitz and Cueva Blanca.

Permission to excavate the site was granted by Mexico's Instituto Nacional de Antropología e Historia; we are particularly grateful to the late José Luis Lorenzo, who greatly expedited our work. The *presidente municipal* of San Pedro y San Pablo Mitla and the *agente* of Unión Zapata ("Loma Larga"), on whose *ejido* land the site is located, showed us great hospitality.

The late Dr. John Paddock of Mexico City College (now Universidad de las Américas) arranged for us to have both lodging and laboratory facilities at the Frissell Museum of Zapotec Art in Mitla. The late director of the museum, Sr. Darío Quero, made sure we had everything we needed.

In the field, artist Nancy Hansen drew all of the chipped stone tools from Gheo-Shih, while Chris Moser developed and printed our black-and-white photographs in his homemade darkroom. Back in the United States, graphic artist Bruce Worden transformed our field drawings and photographs into first-rate illustrations. We are grateful to editor Elizabeth Noll for skillfully turning our manuscript into a book. Our colleague Joyce Marcus took time out from her own research to proofread every word and introduce order into our bibliography.

We are indebted to a series of Mexican colleagues who encouraged our work over the years. Ignacio Bernal, Lorenzo Gamio, Manuel Esparza and Angeles Romero, Ernesto González Licón and Lourdes Márquez Morfín, Linda Manzanilla, and Leonardo López Luján made working in Mexico a delight. Our colleague Nelly Robles García not only facilitated our work on the Archaic, but also convinced UNESCO to declare the sites of the El Fuerte region part of a World Heritage Protected Zone.

Part I

Introduction

Chapter 1

The Discovery of Gheo-Shih

Gheo-Shih is a 1.5 hectare campsite of the Archaic period, located some four kilometers west of the town of Mitla, Oaxaca. It is one of a series of Archaic sites on the lands of the former Hacienda El Fuerte, which took its name from a rocky mesa known as the Mitla Fortress (Figure 1.1).

Our search for Late Pleistocene and Archaic sites in this region began in 1964 and continued in 1966 and 1967. Some of the highlights of this search were the discoveries of Cueva Blanca (OC-30) in 1964, Guilá Naquitz Cave (OC-43) and the Martínez Rockshelter (OC-48) in 1966, and Gheo-Shih (OS-70) in 1967. Gheo-Shih is unique among our Archaic sites because it is an open-air campsite, located on a gentle slope above the alluvium of the Río Mitla (Figure 1.2).

The 1967 Survey

In 1966, Flannery and Hole succeeded in excavating Guilá Naquitz (Flannery 2009a), Cueva Blanca (Flannery and Hole 2019), and the Martínez Rockshelter (Flannery and Spores 2003). While these caves and rockshelters yielded a wealth of data on the Archaic, Flannery and Hole did not feel that their understanding of the period would be complete without the excavation of an open-air campsite. They suspected, in fact, that Archaic foragers probably spent more time in the open than in caves; previous researchers had simply preferred to dig caves because they tend to have better preservation of flora and fauna.

During his 1964 and 1966 surveys, Flannery had noticed that the lands of the ex-Hacienda El Fuerte had unusual numbers of chipped stone tools on the surface. At first, he believed that the reason might be because the Mitla Fortress was an ancient quarry; it had veins of silicified volcanic tuff that were suitable for tool making. However, project geomorphologist Michael J. Kirkby also informed Flannery that the region of the old hacienda had endured sufficient erosion to expose an old Pleistocene land surface that was not visible elsewhere. Flannery and Hole therefore resolved to see whether an open-air Archaic site could be found within walking distance of the Mitla Fortress.

As university spring terms ended in 1967, student members of the University of Michigan Archaeological Project began to arrive at our field headquarters in Mitla. Included were Suzanne Kitchen from Rice University (now

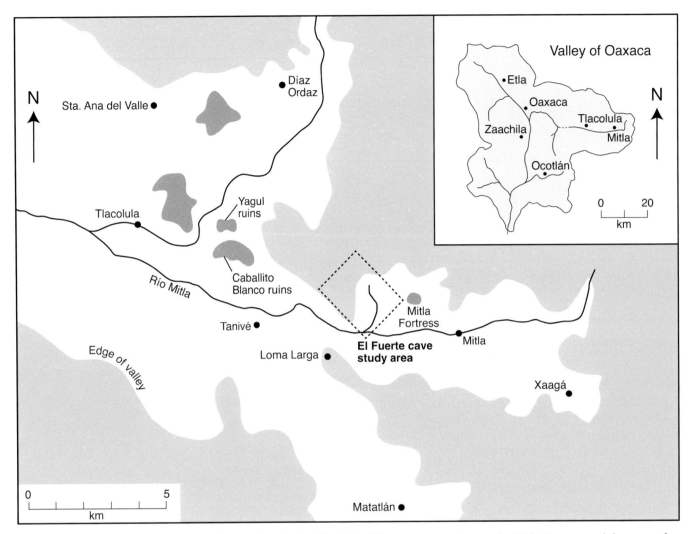

Figure 1.1. The eastern Valley of Oaxaca, showing the relationship of the El Fuerte cave study area, the Mitla Fortress, and the town of Mitla.

Suzanne K. Fish), Richard J. Orlandini from Southern Illinois, Chris L. Moser from Mexico City College, Marcus Winter from Arizona, and Susan H. Lees, Jane Wheeler, and Kathryn Blair Vaughn from Michigan.

Both Flannery and Hole were delayed by various university responsibilities, so they asked all available students to begin walking west from the Mitla Fortress, looking for Archaic remains on the surface. It was during this survey that Gheo-Shih was discovered.

In the late spring of 1967 Gheo-Shih had been cleared of woody vegetation and planted with domestic agaves, which made it easier to find chipped stone tools on the surface. Hole and Flannery went to see the site as soon as they arrived in Mitla, and it was decided that Hole would excavate Gheo-Shih while Flannery tested the Formative site of Barrio del Rosario Huitzo (Flannery and Marcus 2003a).

Picking a Site Name

The Archaic site in the agave field, four kilometers west of Mitla, was designated site OS-70; however, we wanted an actual name for it. Aware that almost every field in the Mitla area has a Zapotec toponym, we asked the farmer who had planted the agaves what he called the place. We wrote down what he said just as we heard it: "Gheo-Shih," or Río de las Jícaras in Spanish. The site's Spanish name—"River of the Gourd Trees"—refers not to the familiar bottle gourd but to the tree gourd, *Crescentia cujete*.

Years later, we were told by a linguist working on Mitla Zapotec that he disagreed with our spelling. The version he preferred would have been "gYew Xi." By then, of course, Gheo-Shih was already in the literature, so we have left it as is.

Figure 1.2. The site of Gheo-Shih, seen from the cliffs to the west. At this point in time the northern two-thirds of the site was planted in parallel rows of agave plants. The rows were flanked by intermittent drainages on the east and west.

The Environmental Setting of Gheo-Shih

The physical environment of the ex-Hacienda El Fuerte has already been described by Kirkby et al. (2009). Figure 1.3 shows a crucial portion of that region, one that includes not only Gheo-Shih but also a dozen of the caves and rockshelters surveyed by the University of Michigan project.

At the bottom of Figure 1.3 we see the Río Mitla, a perennial watercourse, running west from Mitla toward the center of the Oaxaca Valley. We also see that it receives additional water from Gheo-Loh, a stream draining the rocky uplands to the north. The intermittent stream channels feeding Gheo-Loh divide the caves of the El Fuerte region into two groups. To the west, at the top of Figure 1.3, we see six of these caves, including Guilá Naquitz and the Martínez Rockshelter; these sites appear in an ignimbrite (or layered volcanic tuff) cliff at elevations above 1920 m. To the east, in the upper right corner of Figure 1.3, we see six more caves, including Cueva Blanca, occupying an ignimbrite cliff at elevations above 1760 m.

The site of Gheo-Shih can be found in the lower left quadrant of Figure 1.3. It lies at 16° 55' N. Lat., 96° 21' W. long., at an elevation of 1660 m (5445 ft.), only 150 m from the Río Mitla. From Gheo-Shih to Guilá Naquitz Cave is a distance of about 2.5 km, most of it uphill since the difference in altitude is close to 300 m.

This difference in altitude is enough to create a considerable difference in native vegetation between the two sites. Figure 1.4 shows the four vegetation zones and eight facies of vegetation defined for the El Fuerte area by Kirkby et al. Guilá Naquitz Cave lies in the Cassia facies of the Thorn

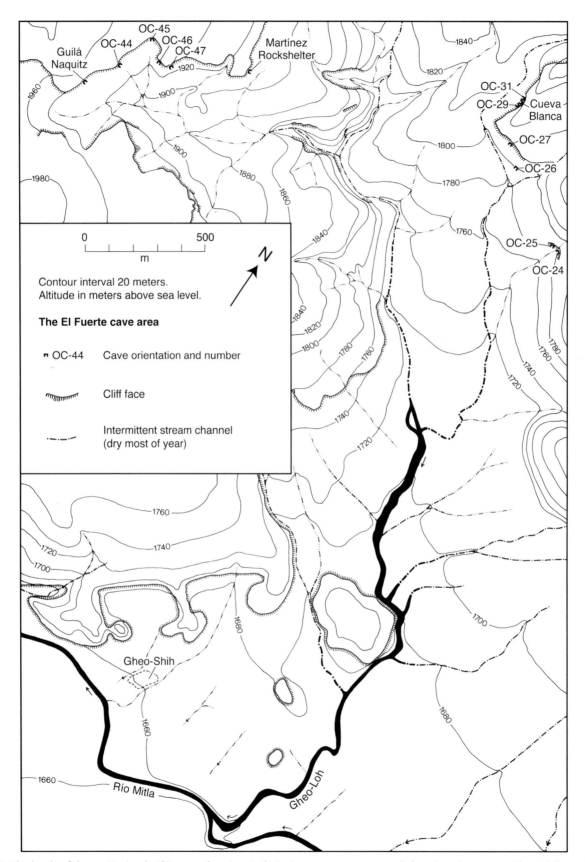

Figure 1.3. The lands of the ex-Hacienda El Fuerte, showing Archaic sites, watercourses, and elevations in meters. Gheo-Shih can be seen in the lower left quadrant of the map.

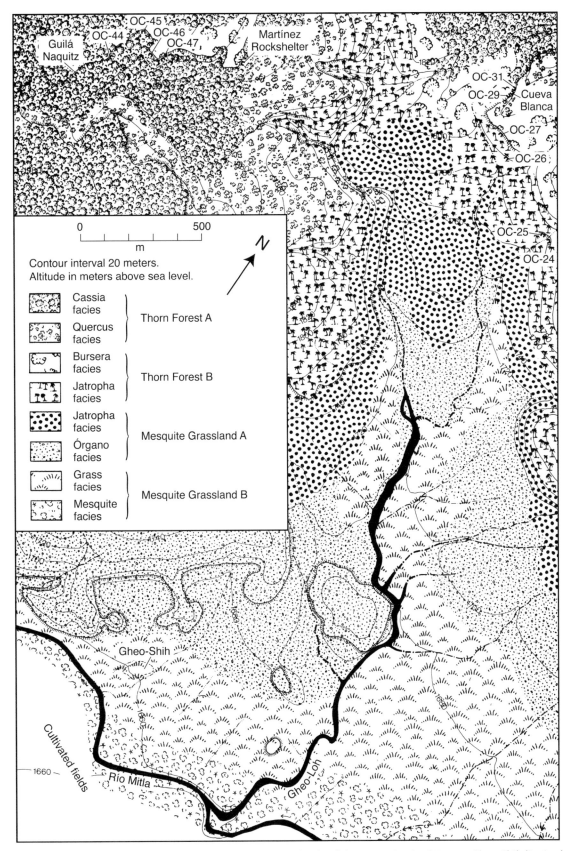

Figure 1.4. Four vegetation zones and eight facies of vegetation on the lands of the ex-Hacienda El Fuerte. Gheo-Shih lies in the grass facies of Mesquite Grassland B.

Forest A Zone, surrounded by tree legumes, columnar cacti, and oak trees. Gheo-Shih, on the other hand, lies today in the grass facies of the Mesquite Grassland B Zone. Kirkby et al. (2009:52) describe Mesquite Grassland B as "all that remains today of the 'original' primary vegetation zone reconstructed by Smith (1978) as mesquite forest." These same authors go on to say that "Where most disturbed by man, [this zone] has a grass facies, with grass dominant, mesquite present but not abundant, and *Jatropha* and *Dodonaea* absent. The open-sir site of Gheo-Shih lies in this barren facies, where human activity will not allow the native vegetation to return" (Kirkby et al. 2009:52–53).

What this analysis means is that Gheo-Shih today occupies a locality where modern land clearance will not allow the original Holocene vegetation to return. Were Gheo-Shih to be left uncultivated for 20 years, it would probably look more like the landscape in Figure 1.5.

Kirkby et al. (2009:53) propose the following:

> Where left undisturbed for a reasonable length of time, a mesquite facies develops that is dominated by *Prosopis juliflora*. The facies characteristically seeks out areas of relatively shallow subsurface water table (less than 5 m), where phreatophytes such as mesquite flourish and form a rather dense growth of trees up to 6 m tall… The pods of these mesquite trees, producing up to 180–200 kg of edible portion per hectare, are one of the main resources of this facies…other important plants include the *rompecapa* or desert hackberry (*Celtis pallida*), whose fruits can be eaten raw…

In other words, at the time Gheo-Shih was first occupied it would likely have been covered with mesquite trees. Some of those trees would have to have been removed in order to allow for the cultivation of gourds, squash, and early maize on the alluvium of the Río Mitla. At the same time, the pods and seeds of the remaining mesquite trees and the fruits of the desert hackberry would likely have been harvested by the Archaic occupants of Gheo-Shih.

Settlement Systems of the Archaic

In our study of settlement patterns in the Mitla Archaic, we have followed the lead of MacNeish (1964, 1972). MacNeish felt that the Archaic sites of Puebla's Tehuacán Valley fell into two general types. At times when resources were abundant at a specific locale, 15–25 individuals might come together to live in what he called a *macroband camp*. This group would remain together at that locale until so much food had been harvested that the point of diminishing returns had been reached.

During seasons of leaner resources, macroband camps broke up into a series of small family groups, who then dispersed throughout the region and foraged on their own. MacNeish referred to the camps made by those groups—often consisting of no more than 4–6 individuals—as *microband camps*.

Such smaller camps might be occupied for anywhere from a few days to most of a season. Once resource conditions improved, various of these family-sized groups might once again join forces to create a larger camp.

In constructing his typology of camps, MacNeish drew on the work of ethnologist Julian Steward (1938, 1955). Steward's analyses of the historic Paiute and Shoshone of the Great Basin revealed that these Native American groups displayed just such a cycle of consolidation and dispersal. They might converge on one spot to engage in large communal hunts of jackrabbit or pronghorn antelope; at other times, they might disperse into smaller groups who harvested pinyon nut groves to which they had usufruct rights. Although no season was without its ritual, these Great Basin foragers saved their largest rituals for the periods when the largest numbers of people were encamped together.

During our earlier work on the Archaic, we added a few more types of sites to MacNeish's scheme: special-purpose camps (Flannery 2003). Such special-purpose sites could include chert or flint quarries, agave roasting camps, and all-male deer hunting camps. The slopes of the Mitla Fortress would be an example of a quarry site; the site of Yuzanú near Yanhuitlán, Oaxaca (Lorenzo 1958) would be an example of an agave-roasting camp; and Zone C of Cueva Blanca has already been interpreted as an all-male hunting camp (Flannery and Hole 2019).

Our guess is that many of these special-purpose camps were made by small groups of people who came from—and later returned to—macroband camps. For example, the proposed all-male camp in Zone C of Cueva Blanca may have been founded by a small group of deer hunters who left a macroband camp for a few days, killed a deer or two, and later returned with the meat.

We were eager to excavate Gheo-Shih because, as a large, open-air Archaic campsite, it had the potential to fill a lacuna in our understanding of the Mitla Archaic. For one thing, its location near the alluvium of the Río Mitla made it likely that early agriculture was one of the activities carried out there. The large size of the site also raised the possibility that its seasonal population might have been greater than the 15–25 persons usually hypothesized for macroband camps;

Figure 1.5. The mesquite facies of Mesquite Grassland B. The mesquite trees in the foreground are growing on the alluvium of the Río Mitla, which is also the best agricultural land in the region. The rocky mesa on the right, roughly a kilometer from the camera, is the so-called Mitla Fortress, a source of silicified tuff for chipped stone tools.

an occasional occupation by 50 people does not even seem unreasonable.

Research at Gheo-Shih

In the chapters that follow we outline the research carried out at Gheo-Shih in the summer of 1967: first, a systematic surface pickup of the entire site; second, a program of systematic depth-probing and test-pitting; third, the excavation of areas where the depths of deposits seemed promising; and finally, preliminary analysis of the materials recovered.

We should say a bit about the differences between a dry cave and an open-air campsite. On the one hand, we recovered more chipped stone from Gheo-Shih than from any of our other Archaic sites, including so-called "tools to make other tools." On the other hand, we recovered no plants or animal bones at all. Millennia of exposure to the elements had destroyed everything organic, leaving neither food remains nor bone tools. Gheo-Shih had also been plowed, an activity not seen at any cave or rockshelter. This meant that the uppermost 10 to 20 cm of the site were often so disturbed that they had to be removed before we could excavate the intact Archaic deposits.

On the plus side, it turned out that most of Gheo-Shih dated to 6000–4000 BC in conventional radiocarbon years. This was a Middle Archaic period for which our cave sites had provided few data. Gheo-Shih therefore became the type site for the Jícaras phase, a period for which we borrowed the Spanish name for the site. One of the type fossils for that phase was the Pedernales atlatl point, some 23 examples of which were recovered from Gheo-Shih. By a wonderful stroke of luck, a small group of early maize cobs from Guilá Naquitz Cave has been radiocarbon dated to the Jícaras phase (Piperno and Flannery 2001). We therefore consider it possible that one reason so many foragers converged on Gheo-Shih was that they could grow maize, squash, gourds, and other early cultivars on the alluvium of the nearby Río Mitla. We will explore this possibility further in Chapter 13.

Chapter 2

The Systematic Surface Pickup

One of the first tasks facing Hole at Gheo–Shih was to determine the limits of the site. Adding to the difficulty of that task was the fact that the scatter of artifacts on the surface was being continuously expanded by erosion. For practical reasons, he decided to use natural landmarks to define the limits of the site wherever possible.

For the northern limit of Gheo-Shih, Hole chose the dirt road he and Flannery had used in 1966 to reach Cueva Blanca. This road began at a ford on the Río Mitla and ended at an old irrigation dam near the cave. It passed conveniently near the northern limits of Archaic material on the surface of Gheo-Shih and was, in fact, the road by which his crew reached the site every day. (To be sure, we occasionally found Archaic projectile points on the surface of the road.)

For the eastern and western limits of the site, Hole used the two intermittent drainages that flanked it (Figure 2.1). These drainages were dry in winter, but carried runoff water in the summer rainy season; this moisture was enough to support woody vegetation.

The most difficult boundary to establish lay to the south, where two geological processes were at work. For one thing, erosion there was exposing the indurated Pleistocene alluvium on which the site had been founded. At the same time, recent alluvium from the Río Mitla was encroaching on the site from the south. Of all the site boundaries, therefore, this was the most arbitrary.

Notwithstanding all the problems outlined above, Hole calculated that Gheo-Shih once covered more than 14,000 square meters, or nearly 1.5 hectares. Clearly, therefore, it qualifies as a *macroband camp* in MacNeish's terms (MacNeish 1964, 1972). We are not convinced, however, that there was ever a moment when all 1.5 ha were occupied. We see Gheo-Shih as a favored locality to which as many as 25–50 forager-farmers returned year after year, making it a palimpsest of overlapping campsites rather than one giant camp.

Surface Pickup

Once Hole had decided on the limits of the site, his next task was to determine where to excavate. In order to make the

Figure 2.1. Systematic surface pickup of Gheo-Shih. In this photograph, a crew of 12 is searching for artifacts on the southern part of the site. Readily visible are the two intermittent drainages flanking the site, the rows of cultivated agaves, and the whitish patches where Pleistocene alluvium has been exposed by erosion.

most informed decision, he decided to grid the entire site and carry out a systematic surface pickup. Accordingly, his crew laid out the grid of 928 5 x 5 m squares shown in Figure 2.2. This grid was oriented to magnetic north. Running from north to south along the west edge of the grid were numbers from 1 through 32. Running from west to east along the north edge of the grid were the letters of the alphabet. Hole had originally planned to use only the letters from A to V; after finding additional material on the surface, however, he decided that the grid needed to be expanded. He therefore added six squares (AA to FF) to the west of A, and one square (X) to the east of V. Now the crew could refer their surface finds to squares with labels such as C18, N4, or BB25.

The systematic surface pickup of Gheo-Shih was carried out by a crew that, on any given day, might involve 10–12 persons (Figures 2.1, 2.3). Included were most of the student participants of the University of Michigan project, plus a group of Zapotec workmen from Mitla. All of the latter were familiar with chipped stone tools, since they had worked at Cueva Blanca during the previous year (Flannery and Hole 2019).

Whenever possible, artifacts such as projectile points, bifaces, manos, etc. were plotted where they lay on the ground. To be sure, some tools only became typologically recognizable after they had been washed in our lab in Mitla; those tools were simply recorded by square. In the end, only 563 of the 928 squares yielded diagnostic tools.

The systematic surface pickup of Gheo-Shih recovered 10,592 items of stone (retouched chert tools, debitage, and fragments of ground stone), as well as 2007 sherds. The sherds, most of which were found near the southern limits of the site, largely belonged to the Monte Albán V period; included were both typical G3M graywares (widespread Postclassic grayware) and Yanhuitlán Red-on-Cream. Other Late Postclassic artifacts included a copper bell (Figure 2.4) and several backed and truncated obsidian blades from a *macana* or indigenous broadsword. We should stress that we found no evidence of actual Monte Albán V occupation when testing or excavating Gheo-Shih; it is simply the case that Late Postclassic sherds are ubiquitous on the surface anywhere within five kilometers of Mitla (Flannery and Marcus 2003b).

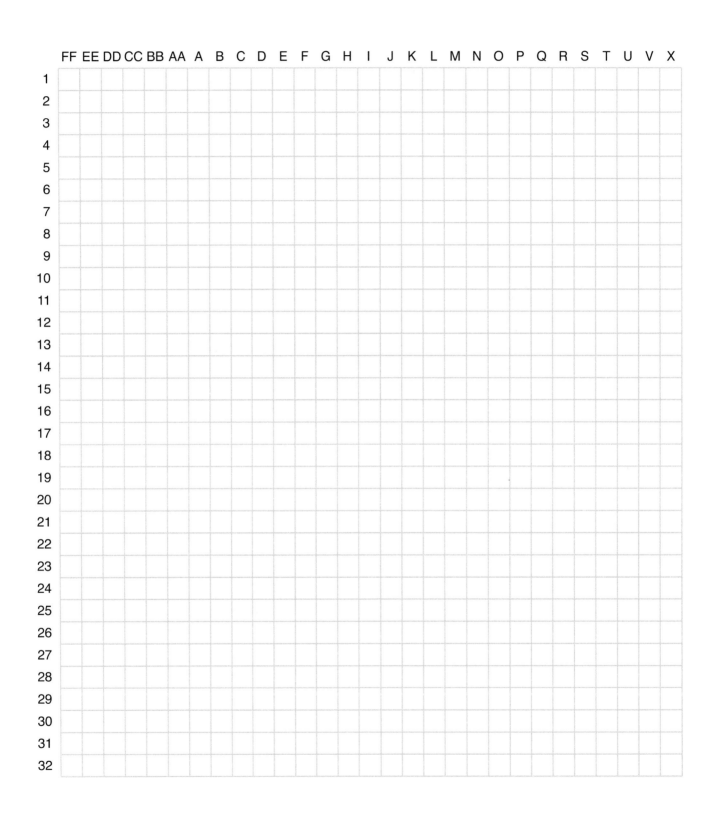

Figure 2.2. The grid of 5 x 5 m squares used for the systematic surface pickup at Gheo-Shih. (North is at the top of the page for all grids.)

Figure 2.3. A view of Gheo-Shih from the cliffs to the northwest. Two archaeologists are visible in the center of the photograph, trying to establish the southern limits of the site. The line of trees in the distance follows the course of the Río Mitla.

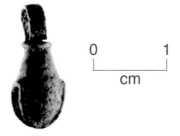

Figure 2.4. A copper bell of the Monte Albán V period. Although Postclassic artifacts were scattered over the surface of the site, no actual occupation from that period was found.

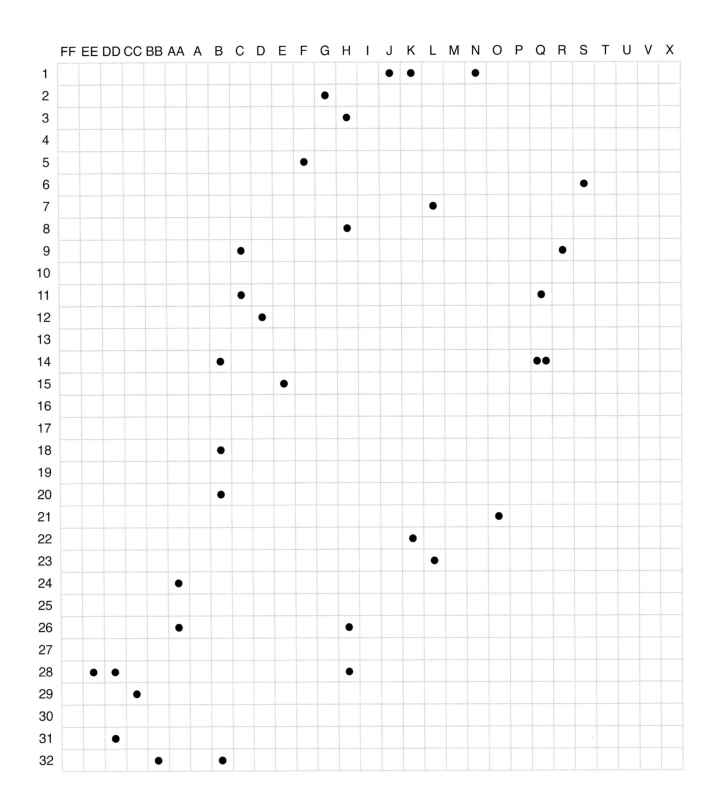

Figure 2.5. The distribution of projectile points, or fragments thereof, recovered from the surface of Gheo-Shih while the 5 x 5 m grid was in effect. (Many of these points can be seen in Chapter 7.)

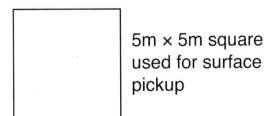

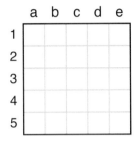

Figure 2.6. Diagram showing the way each 5 x 5 m square used for surface survey could be divided into twenty-five 1 x 1 m squares for the purpose of testing and excavation.

The Relationship of Surface and Subsurface Material

At the time we excavated Gheo-Shih we were already aware of Lewis R. Binford's 1963 discoveries at Hatchery West, Illinois, although they had not yet been published. At the site of Hatchery West, Binford et al. (1970) were interested in finding prehistoric houses. Presuming that surface remains might serve as a guide, they surface-collected the site intensively and drew contour lines reflecting the sherd density. As it happened, the areas of highest sherd density on the surface overlay subsurface middens; the houses were found below areas of lower sherd density.

The Hatchery West report is a warning that the relationship between surface and subsurface remains can be complex and even counterintuitive. To see how this warning applies to Gheo-Shih, we need only look at the locations of projectile points (and fragments thereof) recovered by our surface pickup (Figure 2.5). When one plots those 33 points or point fragments, their distribution takes the form of an ellipse, 30 m long from north to south and 10 m wide from east to west. The reason for this elliptical distribution became apparent once we began excavating the site (see Chapter 3). The interior of the ellipse was an area of slightly higher ground, where erosion was minimal; in contrast, the edges of the ellipse were areas where seasonal flooding from the two intermittent drainages was gradually eroding the Archaic deposits. The areas with the highest surface density of points were therefore not the most promising localities for excavation, but the very opposite: they were areas where many of the Archaic deposits had almost eroded away. Nowhere was this more the case than in the southwest corner of the site (Squares EE28 to AA32), where we tried to establish Excavation Area B (Chapter 3).

Preparations for Testing and Excavations

After all the artifacts from the surface pickup had been washed, labeled, and assigned to a type, Hole and his crew were ready to begin an equally systematic program of testing. For excavation, of course, the 5 x 5 m squares they had used for surface survey were far too large. Figure 2.6 shows how this grid was downsized. Each 5 x 5 m square was divided into twenty-five 1 x 1 m squares. Small case letters (a–e) were used to establish five west-to-east columns; numbers (1–5) were used to establish five north-to-south rows. In this way, a 5 x 5 m square called G27 could be divided into twenty-five 1 x 1 m squares called G27/a1 through G27/e5. These smaller squares were the ones used for testing and excavation. To further distinguish these two units, we use a capital "S" for 5 x 5 m squares and a lower case "s" for 1 x 1 m squares.

Chapter 3

Systematic Testing and the Establishment of Areas A and C

Once the systematic surface pickup of Gheo-Shih was complete, and Hole had had a chance to wash, label, and classify all the artifacts collected, his crew began to prepare for excavation. The first order of business was to decide exactly which areas of the 1.5 ha site should be excavated.

Probes

In the course of our surface pickup it had become clear that the edges of the site were often eroded down to the ancient land surface on which the site's first occupants settled. Owing to this erosion, these marginal areas often featured some of the highest surface densities of artifacts; however, they were unsuitable for excavation because they offered no hope of finding tools in situ.

It was decided to probe the central portions of the site in order to determine where the depth might be greatest. This program of probing was under the supervision of Suzanne Kitchen. The probes used had been made from iron reinforcing rods by a local blacksmith, who gave each probe a sharp lower end and bent the upper end over so that it could be hammered into the ground.

After a period of experimentation, Kitchen decided on the strategy of probing the exact center of each 5 x 5 m grid square. Fortunately, the probes passed easily through the upper deposits and encountered resistance when their points reached the ancient land surface. This allowed Kitchen to locate areas where the deposits were 40 cm deep or deeper; such areas tended to have fewer artifacts on the surface, presumably because they had suffered less erosion. They then became targets for actual 1 x 1 m test pits.

Systematic Test Pits

Each test pit made at Gheo-Shih corresponded to one of the 1 x 1 m squares established within the original 5 x 5 m squares

Figure 3.1. Excavation of the test pits that led to the creation of Area A. In the background we see dirt from the test pits being screened.

used for our surface pickup (Figures 3.1, 3.2). Among the most informative early test pits were the following 63 1 × 1 m squares:

B12/a2, B12/d2
C12/b2, C12/e2, C13/a2, C13/d2,
C14/b2, C14/e2, C15/a2, C15/d2, C16/b2, C16/e2
C17/e1, C18/e1, C19/e1, C20/e1, C21/e1, C22/e1
D12/c2, D13/b2, D14/c2, D15/b2, D16/c2, D17/e1
D18/e1, D19/e1, D20/e1, D21/e1, D22/e1
E12/a2, E12/d2, E13/c2, E14/a2, E14/d2, E15/c2
E16/a2, E16/d2, E17/e1, E18/e1, E19/e1
E20/e1, E21/e1, E22/e1
F12/b2, F12/e2, F13/a2, F13/d2
F14/b2, F14/e2, F15/a2, F15/d2
F16/b2, F16/e2, F17/e1, F18/e1, F19/e1
F20/e1, F21/e1, F22/e1
G21/e5, G29/b2
J14/a2, J14/e2

One of the things we learned from the test pits was that surface remains were not necessarily reliable indicators of the depth or undisturbed nature of the deposits. For example, the first two test pits we excavated were J14/a2 and J14/e2, located near the center of the site, where there were high concentrations of material on the surface. At a depth of only 10 cm, both test pits encountered a layer of dense, dark clay alluvium; only 5 cm below this was the indurated Pleistocene alluvium that constituted sterile soil at the site. It appeared that the large amounts of surface material were the result of erosion, and few artifacts were recovered from these test pits.

The results were quite different in Test Pit G29/b2. There the upper levels of the test pit (after removal of the plow zone) appeared to constitute intact deposits of the Archaic period. Some 40–50 cm below the surface we reached the indurated sand alluvium that constituted sterile soil; to our surprise, however, we came upon a line of boulders that clearly had been brought in from elsewhere

Figure 3.2. The laying out of a series of test pits in Area A. On the right, we see that the plow zone has already been removed.

and set in place. Our desire to find the limits of this manmade boulder line led us to open additional squares in every direction. This part of the site eventually became Excavation Area A (Figures 3.4, 3.19), and the line of boulders turned out to be part of Feature 1 (see Chapter 4).

We eventually identified two more areas of the site —Areas B and C—that we thought might be worthy of excavation. Area B was eventually discontinued, but Area C (initially discovered by Test Pits D14/c2 and E14/d2) was extensively excavated and contributed important data.

Area A

Once the intriguing boulder line had been revealed by Test Pit G29/b2, Hole and Kitchen staked out an additional series of 1 x 1 m squares in the immediate vicinity. They then began excavating alternate squares, temporarily leaving the intervening squares unexcavated so that they could examine their profiles. Unfortunately, owing to extensive leaching and recent agave cultivation, these profiles were not particularly informative. The crew was therefore forced to excavate by arbitrary 10 cm levels, screening as they went (Figure 3.3).

The crew eventually found that there were in fact two parallel boulder lines, spaced 7 m apart and extending NW–SE for 20 m. As a result, they wound up excavating 451 m^2 in this part of the site, the equivalent of 16 of the 5 x 5 m squares they had used for the surface pickup (Figure 3.4). Hole designated this locality Area A, and it became the largest of the areas excavated at Gheo-Shih.

The stratigraphy of Area A was as follows. Its basal level, which included the parallel lines of boulders, was founded on the old land surface that Michael Kirkby had identified as indurated sand alluvium from a Pleistocene stage of the Río Mitla. This ancient alluvial surface was not completely level; it featured occasional depressions that

Figure 3.3. Looking northeast over Area A during the course of excavation. One line of boulders has already been exposed to the level of sterile soil; however, portions of the Jícaras phase component still remain to be excavated. In the background, dirt from the excavation is being screened.

had filled with more recent soil. On this slightly undulating surface, the early occupants of Gheo-Shih had constructed what appeared to be a ritual feature of some kind: an area 7 m wide and 20 m long, swept clean of artifacts and set off from its surroundings by two parallel lines of boulders (see Chapter 4). To either side of this ritual feature there were concentrations of firecracked rocks, pebbles, and chert debitage. Luckily, Hole was able to find a small deposit of burned twigs associated with the ritual feature; these twigs yielded two radiocarbon dates with a calibrated two-sigma range of 7630–7570 BC, placing the basal level of Area A in the late Naquitz phase (see Chapter 12).

The crew found numerous soil discolorations that they suspected might be postmolds in this basal level. However, all of them turned out to be rodent burrows when cross-sectioned (Figures 3.5, 3.6).

Stratigraphically above this basal level was a later component that, depending on the square involved, varied from 5 to 25 cm in thickness. This component was dated by projectile point typology to the Middle Archaic Jícaras phase (6000–4000 BC). Unfortunately, the crew recovered no charcoal from this component that could be used for radiocarbon dating, nor did this Jícaras phase component display any changes in color or texture that would have allowed for any kind of division into smaller stratigraphic units. The Jícaras phase component of Area A did, however, produce a sample of 581 chipped stone tools, which tell us a great deal about the activities carried out on that part of the site (Figure 3.7).

Area B

Near the southwest corner of the site of Gheo-Shih lay an area where a large number of projectile points and bifaces had been recovered from the surface (see Figure 2.5). Even

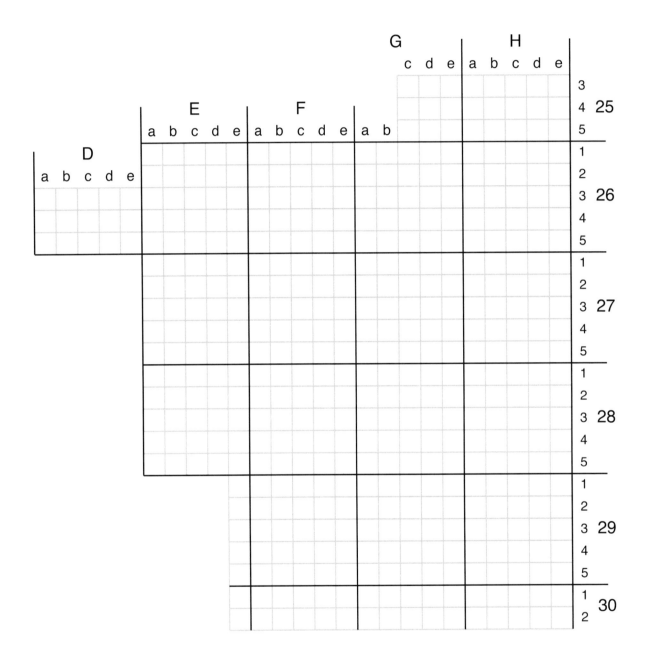

Figure 3.4. The grid of 1 x 1 m squares established for Area A at Gheo-Shih. (North is at the top of the page for all grids.)

Figure 3.5. A workman in Area A cross-sections a soil discoloration to determine whether or not it is a posthole.

Figure 3.6. Here we see a cross-sectioned soil discoloration that turned out to be a rodent burrow. The circular area of discoloration can be seen on the edge of the pit. From there, the rodent burrow descends toward the bottom of the pit, then turns toward the camera.

Figure 3.7. A Pedernales point, found in situ in square H25/a5 of Area A's Jícaras phase component. Surrounding it are stones left in place on pedestals. The arrow points to magnetic north, and the scale is in centimeters.

though several initial test pits had suggested an inverse relationship between stratigraphic depth and the density of surface artifacts, the crew decided to test this area further. Their hope was to recover large numbers of chipped stone tools in situ.

Hole's work in this area, which he designated Area B, began with the probing of Squares CC29, BB29, and AA29. The results of this probing was encouraging enough so that his crew divided these 5 x 5 m squares into 1 x 1 m squares and began to excavate alternate squares (Figure 3.8). Unfortunately, the depth of deposit turned out to be so disappointing, and the artifacts so few, that Hole abandoned Area B after only 29 1 x 1 m squares had been excavated.

Area B did produce several features of recent origin. In squares AA29/d5 and AA29/e5 the crew found two deep postholes, one of which still had wood remaining in it. Several nearby squares still held the root systems of modern agave plants. Finally, just to the south of Area B the crew investigated a line of stones that, based on its stratigraphic context, had to be of recent origin. They eventually concluded that the stones were part of a small check dam and the postholes were from a farmer's field house; it seems possible that this farmer had been using one of the local intermittent drainages for rainy season floodwater farming.

Area C

There were several reasons why Area C was chosen for excavation. First, the surface pickup in Squares D14 and E14 had produced a large number and variety of artifacts. Second, Kitchen's probing of this part of the site suggested that the soil there was deep enough to ensure recovery of material from below the plow zone. In fact, a number of probes had suggested the presence of an extensive depression, some 50 cm deeper than the average depth to sterile soil; it was hoped that this additional depth would

Figure 3.8. Workmen testing Area B of Gheo-Shih. In the left half of the photograph, one can see that erosion has exposed the sterile Pleistocene alluvium on which the site was founded. Area B proved disappointing and was eventually abandoned.

allow for the discovery of features or structures. Finally, Test Pits D14/c2 and E14/d2 had proved encouraging.

During the second week of August, Hole and Kitchen decided on the limits of what would become Area C. So productive was this area that they eventually wound up excavating 136 1 x 1 m squares (Figure 3.9). Included were all of Squares D14, E14, D15, and E15, plus the easternmost ten 1 x 1 m squares of Square C14; the northernmost ten 1 x 1 m squares of Square D16; the northernmost ten 1 x 1 m squares of Square E16; and a series of six 1 x 1 m squares from Squares F14 and F15.

As usual, the crew began their excavation of Area C by digging alternate squares (Figure 3.10) and piece-plotting significant artifacts (Figure 3.11). Area C did have the

Figure 3.9 (right). The grid of 1 x 1 m squares established for Area C of Gheo-Shih; all were excavated. The six easternmost 1 x 1 m squares (belonging to 5 x 5 m Squares F14 and F15) were discontinued below the upper component (a) of Area C.

Figure 3.10. The excavation of Area C by alternate 1 x 1 m squares. At this point, the workmen are excavating the lower component (b); however, a number of stones from the upper component (a) have been temporarily left on pedestals.

Figure 3.11. A Pedernales point, found in situ in square E15/e1 of Area C's lower component (b).

depth of deposit they had hoped for; unfortunately, owing to millennia of exposure to the elements, its stratigraphy did not provide much in the way of soil color or texture changes. Based on the limited clues at their disposal, the crew assigned the upper 20 cm to one component, which they called "a"; below this they established a lower component, called "b," which extended from 20 cm below the surface to the sterile Pleistocene alluvium.

At no point in their excavation did the crew sense that by separating components a and b, they were arbitrarily dividing one Archaic occupation into two. In addition, when we compare the horizontal distribution of chipped stone tools from components a and b (Chapter 6), we find them sufficiently different to support the conclusion that we are dealing with two different Jícaras phase occupations.

Note that while the excavation of component a involved 136 1 x 1 m squares, the excavation of component b involved only 130 (Figure 3.12). Owing to limitations of time and money, Hole discontinued the six 1 x 1 m squares from Squares F14 and F15 once component a had been fully excavated.

Each stratigraphic component of Area C had its unique features. In component a, for example, the crew found a series of stone-lined hearths or roasting pits; the five best preserved of these were found in Squares D14, D15 and E15 (Figures 3.13–3.16). There may once have been as many as 10 to 12 of these hearths in Area C, but many had been wholly or partially destroyed by subsequent activity. A few had been reduced to no more than clusters of firecracked rocks.

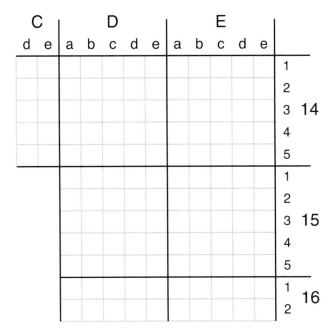

Figure 3.12. The grid of 1 x 1 m squares used for the lower component (b) of Area C. (Note that six fewer squares were excavated in component b.)

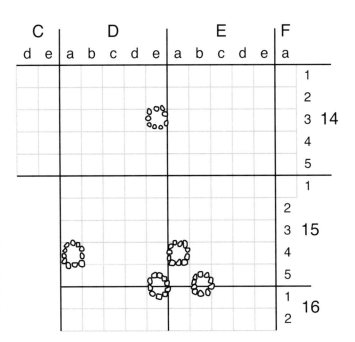

Figure 3.13. The excavation grid for Area C, showing the location of the five best defined hearths or roasting pits found in the upper component (a). The presence of less well defined clusters of firecracked rocks throughout this component suggested that the original number of hearths may have been closer to 10 or 12; many had been damaged by subsequent activity.

Figure 3.14. The remains of a rock-lined hearth or roasting pit in square D14/e3, Area C. These remains, which were found in component a, have been left on pedestals, while adjacent squares were excavated to sterile soil.

Figure 3.15. The remains of a rock-lined hearth or roasting pit in square E15/a4, Area C. These remains, which were found in component a, have been left on a pedestal, while adjacent squares were excavated to sterile soil.

Figure 3.16. A view of the southern part of Area C during excavation. A series of hearths or roasting pits from component a, damaged by subsequent activity, have been left on pedestals, while adjacent squares were excavated to sterile soil. The circular discoloration in the foreground turned out to be a shallow pit dug into sterile soil.

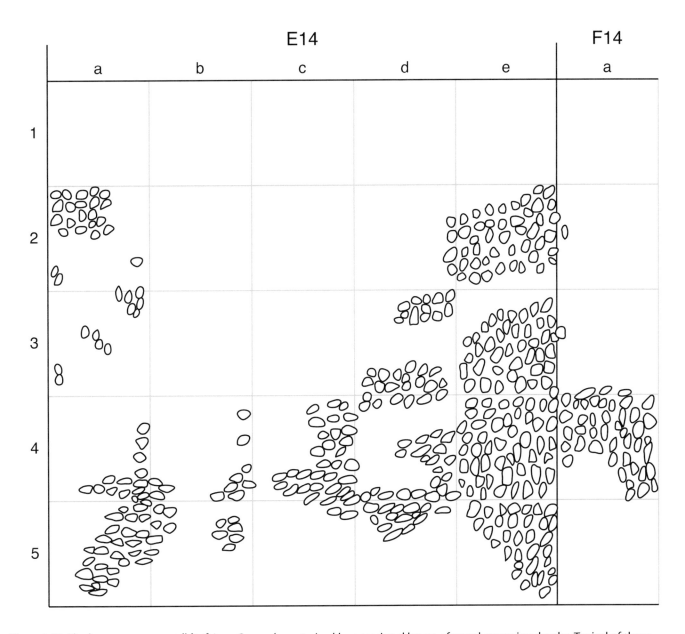

Figure 3.17. The lower component (b) of Area C was characterized by occasional lenses of gravel at varying depths. Typical of those gravel lenses was the one shown here, at a depth of 35 cm in Squares E14 and F14.

We wish that we knew more about the purpose of these hearths and the reason that there were so many on this part of the site. (One possibility, discussed in Chapter 13, is that they were for agave roasting.)

The crew found no reason to doubt that these features dated to the Jícaras phase; certainly, no sherds or other post-Archaic artifacts were found with them. Unfortunately, the crew also found insufficient charcoal (by the standards of 1967) for radiocarbon dating; all they usually recovered were firecracked rocks and blackened or reddened soil.

The lower component (b) also had some unique features. In places, such as in Squares E14 and E15, this component was characterized by lenses of gravel at varying depths (Figures 3.17, 3.18). Had these gravel layers occurred throughout Area C, Hole's crew could have used them as natural breaks between stratigraphic levels; unfortunately, they tended to appear only in certain squares.

In the end, the crew was unable to subdivide component b, which (despite the results of Kitchen's probing) averaged only 20–25 cm in thickness. Nor could they convince themselves that there were significant chronological differences between components a and b; both appeared, based on all the artifacts recovered, to belong to the Jícaras phase.

Summary

After considerable probing and test pitting, Hole's crew ended up excavating two areas of Gheo-Shih: Areas A (451 m^2) and C (361 m^2). Not surprisingly, both these areas lay near the midline of the site, where erosion from the two intermittent drainages was less pronounced (Figure 3.19).

Even before analysis of the artifacts began, it was clear that these two areas were significantly different. Area A had been founded late in the Early Archaic Naquitz phase, and contained a ritual feature of that period. Stratigraphically above that feature was a layer of occupational debris from the Middle Archaic Jícaras phase.

Area C, on the other hand, had no evidence of Naquitz phase occupation. Instead, it seemed to have evidence of two superimposed Jícaras phase occupations, designated components a and b. It appeared that one of the activities carried out in the upper component (a) was the extensive cooking or roasting of some resource, possibly agave hearts.

Subsequent analyses of the artifacts from Areas A and C (Chapters 6, 8, 9, and 10) would reveal other differences among the various components involved. Included were the manufacture of tools using hafted drills and the creation of two different types of stone ornaments.

Figure 3.18. Area C, component b. In the foreground, two workmen remove a gravel lens that has been left on a pedestal. The squares in the background have been excavated to sterile soil.

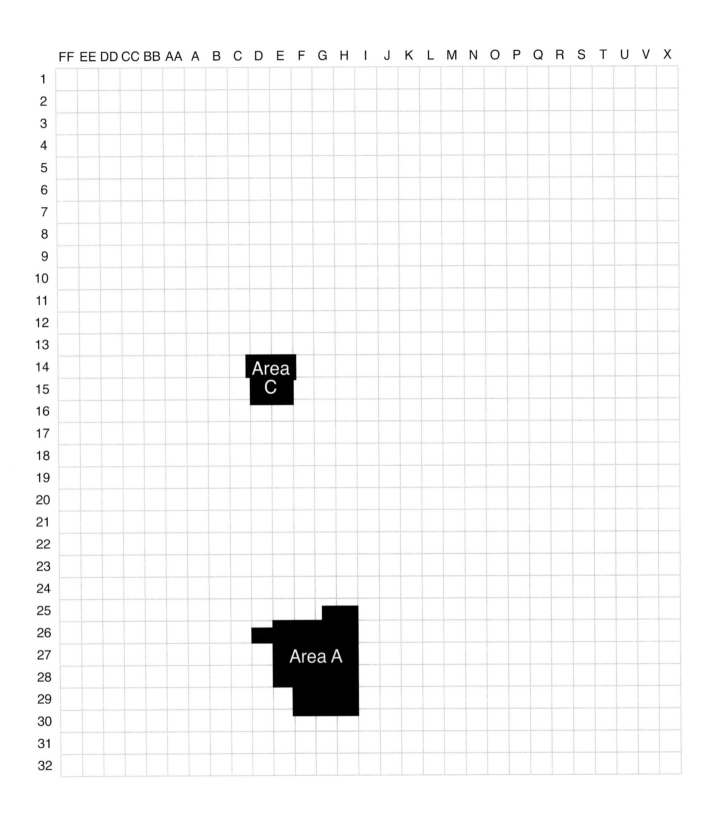

Figure 3.19. The location of Areas A and C within the grid of 5 x 5 m squares created for the systematic surface pickup of Gheo-Shih.

Chapter 4

A Naquitz Phase Ritual Feature from Area A

One of the motivations behind our excavation of Gheo-Shih was to learn what types of shelters were built by the occupants of Archaic open-air sites. Would they be ephemeral huts or windbreaks, pit dwellings, or wattle-and-daub houses? Was the nuclear family the unit of residence, or did extended families live together under one roof?

Once we began excavating Jícaras phase levels, we realized that it would take extraordinary luck to find items like postmolds or burned thatch, given the millennia of rainfall, leaching, and erosion that Gheo-Shih had endured. The last thing we expected is that we would find a relatively intact ritual feature, but that is exactly what happened when we reached the basal level of Area A.

In this chapter we look in detail at Feature 1 of Gheo-Shih, the cleared, boulder-lined ritual space resting on sterile soil in Area A (Figure 4.1). Figure 4.2 shows every boulder, pebble, and chert waste flake that lay in situ on the sand alluvium below Area A. By comparing Figure 4.2 of this chapter to Figure 3.4 of Chapter 3, the reader can see how Feature 1 fits within our 1 x 1 m grid for Area A, a grid that Hole expanded in several directions in order to expose as much of the feature as possible.[1]

Project geomorphologist Michael Kirkby (personal communication, 1967) concluded that sterile soil in Area A was a layer of indurated, sandy alluvium, left by a Pleistocene stage of the Río Mitla. On this ancient surface, the archaic occupants of Gheo-Shih laid out two parallel lines of boulders, running NW–SE for 20 m and spaced 7 m apart (Figure 4.3). The 140 m² enclosed space had been swept clean of artifacts; however, to either side of the boulder-lined feature there were scatters of debris. At least one of these

1. No one in Oaxaca had ever seen anything like Feature 1, and initial speculation about it was wide-ranging. Some of our colleagues from the Frissell Museum even asked if the feature could be a Colonial oxcart road. Geomorphologist Michael Kirkby laid this idea to rest. He explained that Feature 1 was founded on a Pleistocene land surface and sealed below Middle Archaic deposits. He added that he had found a number of Colonial oxcart roads during his surveys of the valley; none were lined with boulders, none were as narrow as 7 m, and all were deeply rutted by oxcart wheels. Eventually, two radiocarbon dates (Chapter 12) made it clear that Feature 1 was Archaic.

Figure 4.1. The basal level of Area A, seen from the northwest corner of the excavation. The boulder lines in the center of the photo define Feature 1.

scatters, to the northeast of Feature 1, could represent debris from an ephemeral shelter of some kind (Figure 4.4).

While we do not know the purpose for which Feature 1 was created, what it most reminds us of are the kinds of spaces that hunting-gathering groups of the Great Basin cleared for dances, initiation ceremonies, or athletic competitions (Lowie 1915; Steward 1938). In previous publications we have referred to Feature 1 as a "dance ground," which we still consider a useful nickname in spite of the fact that we cannot be positive that that was its purpose.

Given the likely ritual function of Feature 1, we of course wondered if its alignment—roughly 290°, relative to true north—had cosmological significance. In 1991 a University of Michigan student, Jon Bryan Burley, took on this question for Flannery. Burley concluded that the boulder-lined area could be considered to have an alignment of 69°45' west of true north (Burley, personal communication, 1991). If, for the sake of argument, we assume that Feature 1 was aligned to the point at which the sun either rose or set on the day of its construction, Burley concluded that it must have been laid out sometime between late May and early July—a period that brackets the summer solstice. This seems not unreasonable to us, since the most

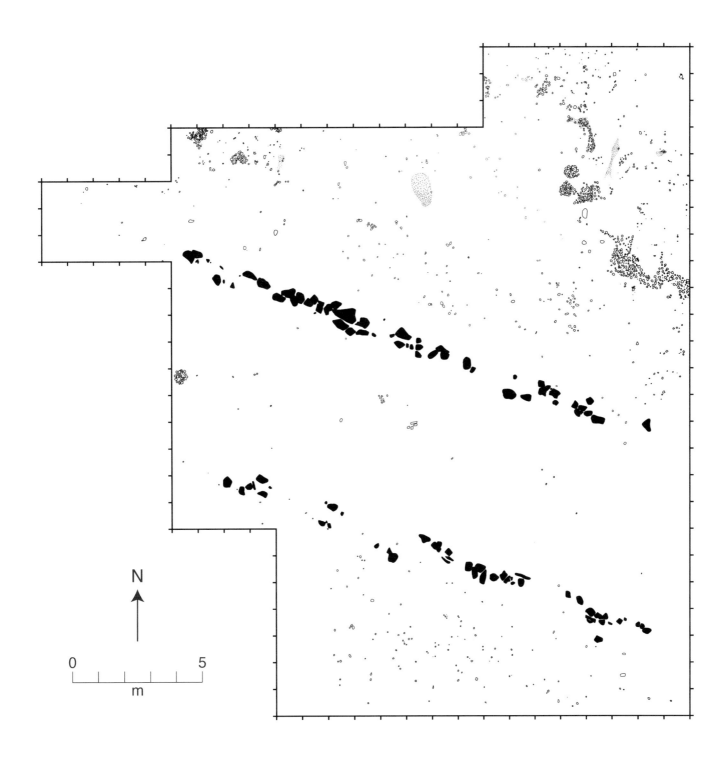

Figure 4.2. A plan drawing of the basal level of Area A. In the center we see the parallel lines of boulders defining Feature 1. In the northeast corner we see a semicircular area of piece-plotted firecracked rocks, pebbles, and chert waste flakes; this scatter of items may indicate the presence of an ephemeral structure of some kind. (The arrow points to magnetic north.)

Figure 4.3. Feature 1, seen from the south. The slender vertical stakes seen in this photo (and Figure 4.1) mark soil discolorations considered possible postmolds. (After careful cross-sectioning, none turned out to be postmolds.) At center left, we see one of the original test pits that led to the creation of Area A.

logical time to camp at Gheo-Shih would have been during the summer rainy season. That is when Archaic crops could have been grown on the alluvium of the Río Mitla; it is also the season when wild resources such as mesquite pods and desert hackberries would have been most abundant.

In the course of his research, Burley also ran across data on the dances and dance grounds employed by the Paiute and Western Shoshone of the Great Basin (see D'Azevedo 1986). For example, the Western Shoshone celebrated times of abundant food supply by holding a ceremony called the Round Dance at their macroband camps (Thomas et al. 1986). One of the important fringe benefits of this dance was that it afforded opportunities for courtship to foragers who spent part of the year in scattered microbands. Liljeblad and Fowler (1986) report that the Paiute of California's Owens Valley set their dance grounds apart with a fence edging; other foraging groups referred to their designated dancing areas as "dance corrals."

We are reluctant to push our analogies for Feature 1 farther than this: hunting-gathering societies of the arid west seem to have had a widespread pattern of setting aside space in their macroband camps for rituals such as dancing, and that space was often delimited by a fence or some other type of boundary.

Because the upper levels of Area A dated to the Jícaras phase—complete with Pedernales atlatl points (Chapter 8)—we expected Feature 1 to date to that phase as well. We were, however, in for a surprise. Hole's crew managed to recover enough charcoal from Feature 1 to provide for two radiocarbon dates with a calibrated two-sigma range of 7720–7560 BC (Chapter 12). This means that Feature 1 not only belonged to the late Naquitz phase, but was essentially contemporaneous with Zone B2 of Guilá Naquitz Cave (Flannery 2009b: Table 1). This puts us in a position to compare and contrast microband and macroband camps of the late Naquitz phase (Chapter 13).

Figure 4.4. The basal level of Area A, seen from the north (Square G25). In the foreground is a scatter of firecracked rocks, pebbles, and chert waste flakes that may indicate the place where an ephemeral shelter once stood.

As for our search for residential structures, it remained frustrating. Hole's crew marked every potential postmold with a slender vertical stake (Figure 4.3) and cross-sectioned it; none of them turned out to be actual postmolds. A semicircle of firecracked rocks, pebbles, and debitage in Squares G25, H25, G26, and H26 may point to the presence of an ephemeral shelter of some kind. The fact that the remains included no postmolds suggests that any shelter present was entirely aboveground.

The presence of Feature 1 at Gheo-Shih suggests that Archaic macroband camps had ritual features found at no microband camp. Of course, it should not surprise us to learn that some rituals, analogous to the Western Shoshone Round Dance, took place only when 25–50 individuals were living together. A microband of 4–6 individuals would have had neither the incentive nor the rationale to construct a feature of this type. It is typical of hunter-gatherers that some rituals were only carried out when enough people were living together to make them worthwhile; and because the timing of macroband camps was likely keyed to resource availability, we suspect that such rituals were carried out on an ad hoc basis, rather than being determined by a calendar of any kind.

Finally, we come to the question of whether such rituals continued during the Jícaras phase. We found no other boulder-lined areas at Gheo-Shih, but given how little of the site we excavated, that is probably not significant. After all, the history of ritual in Oaxaca is that, over time, it increased in size and complexity (Flannery and Marcus 2015).

Part II

The Jícaras Phase Artifacts

Chapter 5

Chipped Stone Tools: The Typology

Hundreds of chipped stone tools were recovered during the systematic surface pickup of Gheo-Shih. More than a thousand were recovered during the excavations that followed.

Sources of Raw Material

As was the case with the chipped stone assemblages from Guilá Naquitz and Cueva Blanca, the majority of the chipped stone tools were of secondarily silicified ignimbrite (volcanic tuff). A logical source for this material was the so-called Fortress of Mitla, an ignimbrite mesa within easy walking distance of Gheo-Shih (Holmes 1897; Whalen 2009; Williams and Heizer 1965). Veins of silicified tuff are widespread in the Fortress, which served as a quarry throughout Oaxaca prehistory. It is also the case, however, that cobbles and pebbles of silicified tuff are readily available in the beds of intermittent drainages in the piedmont north of Gheo-Shih.

A smaller percentage of the chipped stone tools were made from silicified sedimentary rocks. In this case, the raw material likely came from an area of sandstones and marls some five to seven kilometers south of Gheo-Shih, and on the opposite side of the Río Mitla (Whalen 2009: Figure 7.1).

Least common among the raw materials used at Gheo-Shih were fine-grained cherts and chalcedonies, whose origins lay in limestone formations. Whalen (2009) has identified a number of those sources within the Valley of Oaxaca. The nearest to Gheo-Shih lie 25 kilometers to the northwest near Rojas de Cuauhtémoc, still within the Tlacolula arm of the valley. By far the finest raw material available, however, was chalcedony from Peña de Matadamas in the Etla arm of the valley. This source lies 45–55 kilometers away, and we calculate that procuring it would have involved traveling for a day and a half, camping at the quarry, and making a return trip of another day and a half. Presumably owing to the labor involved in procuring this chalcedony, it seems to have been reserved for the best-made bifacial tools, such as projectile points.

Finally, we should mention that no obsidian was present in the Archaic deposits at Gheo-Shih, or for that matter, in the Archaic deposits of any of our caves and rockshelters (Flannery and Hole 2019; Hole 2009).

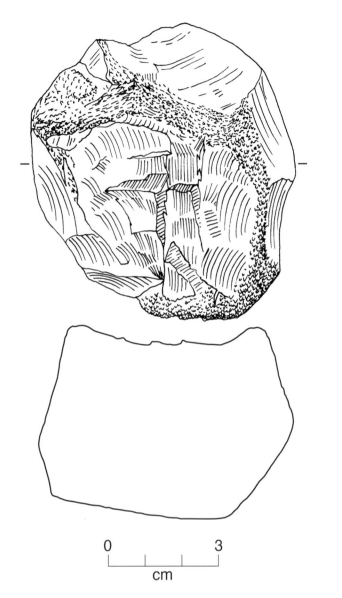

Figure 5.1. A hammerstone from the Jícaras phase component of Area A.

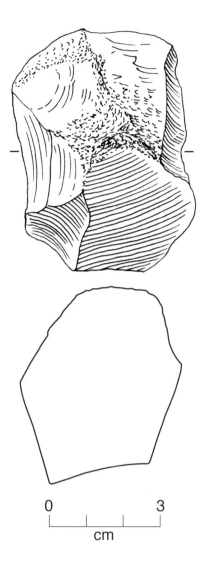

Figure 5.2. A hammerstone from the lower component (b) of Area C.

Tools for Basic Flake Production

Hammerstones (Figures 5.1–5.4)

Most hammerstones were chunks of silicified volcanic tuff, presumably from nearby sources such as the Mitla Fortress; given the uses to which they were put, it would not have been worthwhile using finer raw material. While many hammerstones were undoubtedly used to strike flakes from cores, their horizontal distribution (Chapter 6) indicates that they were also used for pounding other materials.

Some hammerstones were irregularly shaped, possibly as a result of having been discarded at an early stage of use. Others had been used for so long that they became almost spherical, and still others had split during use. In at least a few cases, it appears that the occupants of Gheo-Shih had turned exhausted flake cores into hammerstones.

Typical flake cores (Figures 5.5–5.9)

The flake cores typical of the Naquitz and Jícaras phases were chunks of silicified ignimbrite, silicified sedimentary rock, or chert that had one or more platforms from which

Chipped Stone Tools: The Typology

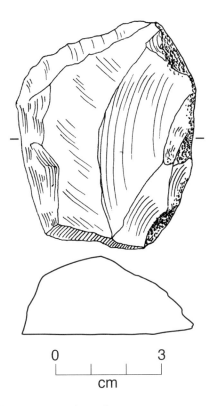

Figure 5.3. A hammerstone from the upper component (a) of Area C.

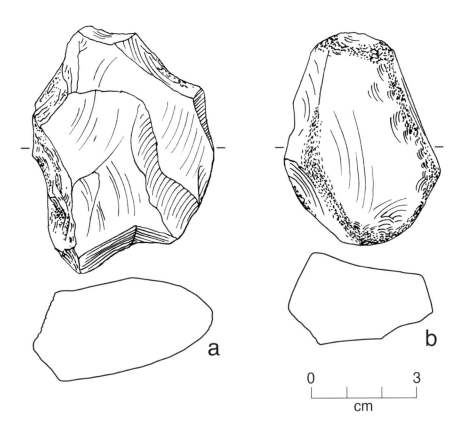

Figure 5.4. Two hammerstones from the Jícaras phase component of Area A.

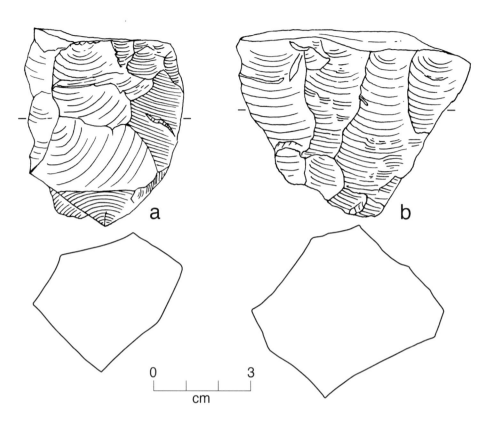

Figure 5.5. Two flake cores from the Jícaras phase component of Area A.

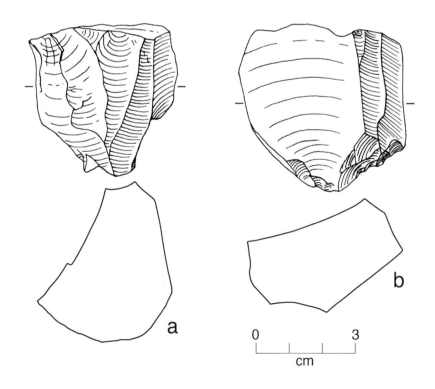

Figure 5.6. Two flake cores from the Jícaras phase component of Area A.

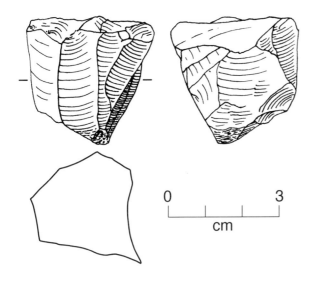

Figure 5.7. A flake core from the Jícaras phase component of Area A.

flakes of a usable size had been struck. Even crude cores could be distinguished from steep denticulate scrapers by the fact that the latter do not display flake scars large enough to have provided the kinds of flakes used as tools by the Archaic foragers.

Our data suggest that prior to the Blanca phase, this type of core was essentially the only one used by the Archaic residents of the Mitla region. During the Blanca phase a second core type—the discoidal core—made its appearance (Flannery and Hole 2019:61). This second core type, however, never became as common as the typical flake core.

Core faces (Figure 5.10a, b)

Core faces are fragments from the sides of flake cores, removed by a blow directed down from the platform. The blow occurred far enough back from the edge of the platform to remove the entire face of the core rather than just one flake.

Core edges (Figure 5.10c, d)

We define a core edge as the edge of a striking platform, removed (in almost all cases) by a blow directed from the side of the core rather than from above.

Debitage

This category includes all those fragments of chipped stone that do not show any signs of retouch (whether deliberate or caused by use) and that cannot be identified as being a

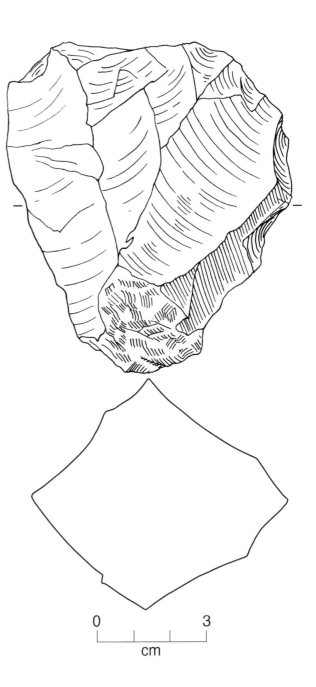

Figure 5.8. A flake core from the lower component (b) of Area C.

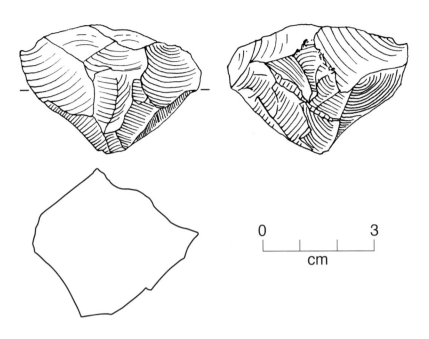

Figure 5.9. A small flake core from Test Pit G21/e5.

specific part of a core. It would probably be misleading to call them all "waste flakes," since some fragments are naturally sharp enough to have been used for light cutting tasks.

Flake Tools

Utilized flakes (Figures 5.11, 5.12)

This tool type consists of flakes or chunks of silicified ignimbrite, silicified sedimentary rock, or chert that have light, shallow chipping limited to part of an edge. The irregular appearance of this chipping suggests that it resulted from light use rather than deliberate retouch. As was the case with both Guilá Naquitz and Cueva Blanca, it appears that whenever the occupants of Gheo-Shih needed to perform some light cutting, they simply picked up any sharp flake they found nearby.

Notched flakes (Figures 5.13–5.15)

This tool type consists of flakes—of any size or shape—that have one or more notches chipped into an edge. The chipping that produced the notch may have been deliberate or caused simply by use on a hard material; some specimens, in fact, may display both deliberate chipping and use wear. A few notched flakes give the impression of being informal spokeshaves, but these are so few in number that we decided not to create a separate tool category for them.

Flakes with bulbar end retouch (Figures 5.16, 5.17)

Within our sample of Archaic sites, this artifact type is unique to Gheo-Shih. These are flakes with deliberate retouch on the end featuring the bulb of percussion. Such tools were not common, but we found enough examples to encourage making them a separate category. It is not clear, however, what function they served.

Crude blades, plain (Figures 5.18–5.20)

We are not convinced that the knappers of Gheo-Shih were trying to make prismatic blades. In the process of striking off thousands of flakes, however, they occasionally produced flakes with parallel sides and a length twice as long as their width. They fit the definition of blades, albeit produced accidentally rather than deliberately. Most of these crude

Chipped Stone Tools: The Typology

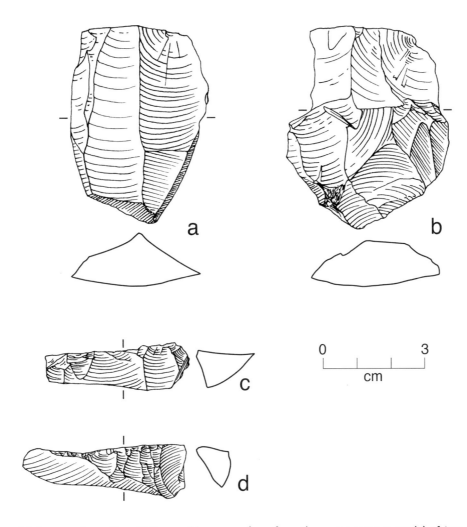

Figure 5.10. Fragments of flake cores from Gheo-Shih. *a* and *b* are core faces from the upper component (a) of Area C. *c* and *d* are core platform edges from Area C (*c* is from the upper component; *d* is from the lower component).

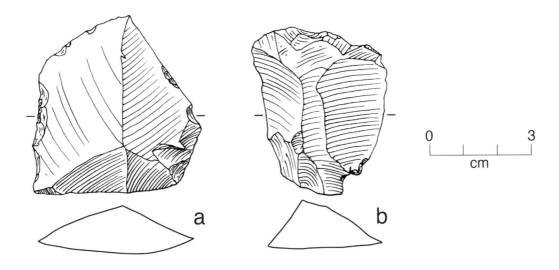

Figure 5.11. Utilized flakes from the upper component (a) of Area C.

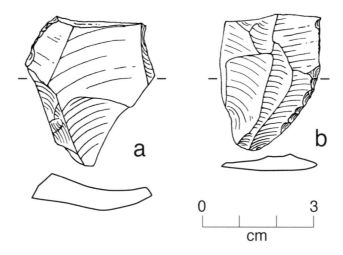

Figure 5.12. Utilized flakes from Area C. *a* is from the upper component; *b* is from the lower component.

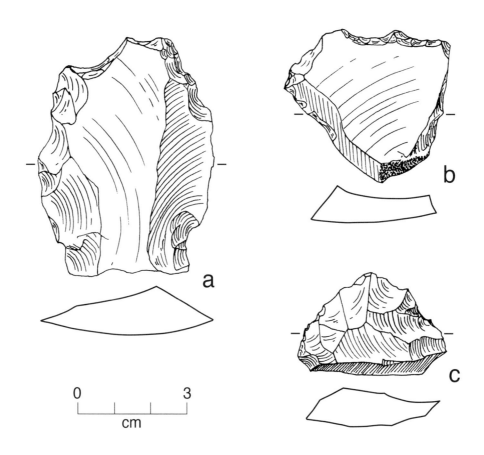

Figure 5.13. Notched flakes from Area C. *a* and *c* are from the lower component. *b* is from the upper component.

Chipped Stone Tools: The Typology

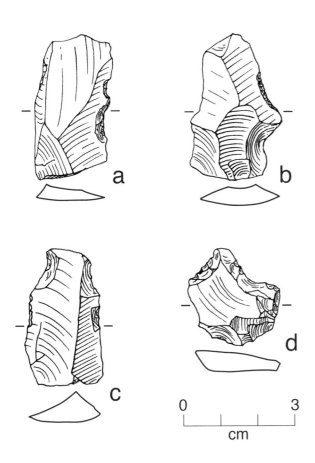

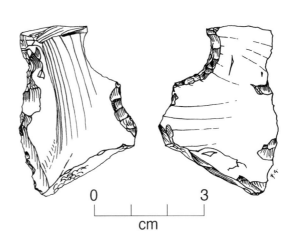

Figure 5.15. A notched flake from the surface (Square C13).

Figure 5.14. Notched flakes from the lower component (b) of Area C. An unusually high number of notched flakes were found in Squares D14–D16, suggesting an activity area.

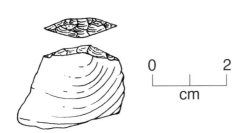

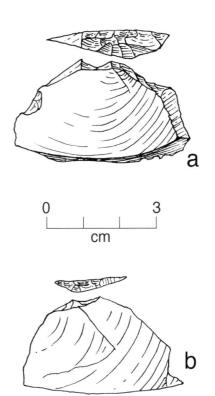

Figure 5.16. A flake with bulbar end retouch from the lower component (b) of Area C.

Figure 5.17. Two flakes with bulbar end retouch from the lower component (b) of Area C.

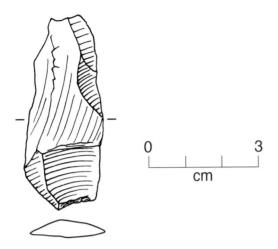

Figure 5.18. A crude blade from the Jícaras phase component of Area A.

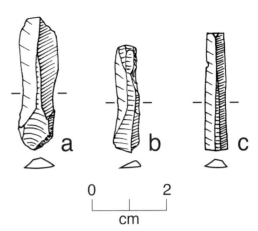

Figure 5.19. Three blades from the Jícaras phase component of Area A.

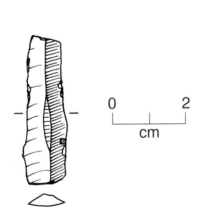

Figure 5.20. A blade from the lower component (b) of Area C.

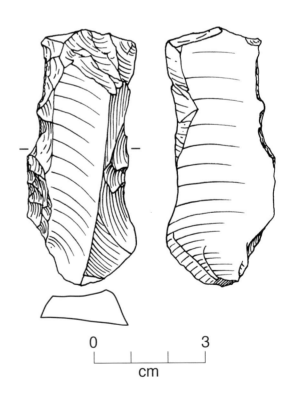

Figure 5.21. A blade with retouch from the lower component (b) of Area C.

blades were unretouched, and probably were used for light cutting tasks.

Crude blades, retouched (Figures 5.21–5.24)

A certain number of crude blades at Gheo-Shih had been deliberately retouched along one or more edges. Similar retouched blades were present at Cueva Blanca (Flannery and Hole 2019:65). At Guilá Naquitz, however, none of the crude blades we found showed signs of deliberate retouch (Hole 2009:109).

Backed blades

A relatively small number of crude blades at Gheo-Shih fit the definition of an Old World "backed blade." These were blades one edge of which had been blunted by steep retouch. Neither Guilá Naquitz nor Cueva Blanca produced backed blades of this type.

Flakes with sheen (Figures 5.25–5.27)

A number of flakes from Gheo-Shih displayed a glossy sheen on one or more edges; similar flakes with sheen were found at Guilá Naquitz (Hole 2009:111–112) and Cueva Blanca (Flannery and Hole 2019:65–69).

As discussed in previous publications, we suspect that one possible cause of this sheen was the prolonged and repetitive trimming of the leaves from an agave heart prior to its roasting. The sawing of an agave's tough, fibrous leaves would be one possible source of the abrasion necessary to produce the sheen. Add to this the fact that the leaf bases of an agave are likely to have a coating of sandy earth, which is also abrasive.

Sickles (Figures 5.28–5.30)

Some of the flakes with sheen from Gheo-Shih would also be classified as crude blades. Their morphological similarity to the familiar sickle blades of the Mediterranean and Near Eastern Neolithic is striking, despite the fact that they cannot possibly have been used to harvest cereals. We have kept these tools separate from Gheo-Shih's larger and more irregular flakes with sheen, because we suspect they may have been used to cut something more delicate than agave leaves.

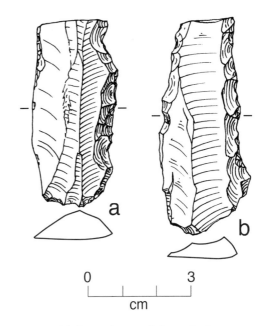

Figure 5.22. Two blades with retouch from the lower component (b) of Area C.

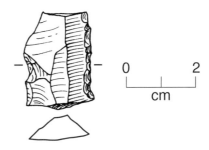

Figure 5.23. A segment of retouched blade from the lower component (b) of Area C.

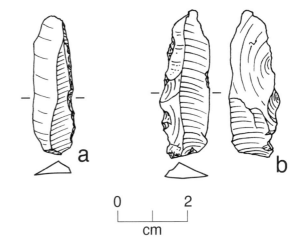

Figure 5.24. Two blades with retouch from Gheo-Shih. *a* was found in the lower component (b) of Area C. *b* is from the surface.

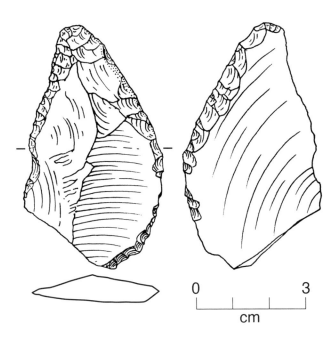

Figure 5.25. A flake with sheen from the lower component (b) of Area C. The area of edge polish is indicated by light stipple.

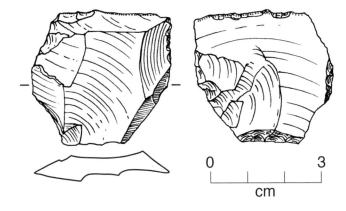

Figure 5.26. A flake with sheen from the Jícaras phase component of Area A. The area of edge polish is indicated by light stipple.

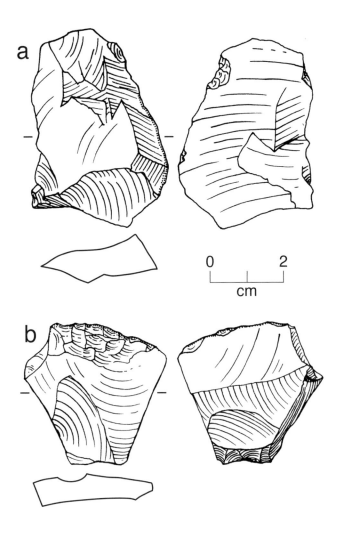

Figure 5.27. Two flakes with sheen from the lower component (b) of Area C. The area of edge polish is indicated by light stipple.

Choppers/Knives

Choppers (Figure 5.31)

These are large flakes, chunks, or nodules of silicified volcanic tuff or sandstone whose edges have been given coarse, sinuous bifacial chipping. Their weight and size suggest that they were used for relatively heavy tasks, such as butchering deer.

At both Guilá Naquitz and Cueva Blanca we have called such tools "choppers/knives," because it appeared that some could have been used either for chopping or cutting. The specimens from Gheo-Shih mostly appear to be chopping tools.

Scrapers

End scrapers (Figures 5.32–5.39)

These artifacts are flakes with one end blunted by steep retouch; the retouched edge is usually convex in outline. While end scrapers were present at all the Archaic sites

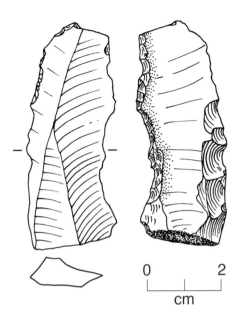

Figure 5.28. A sickle from the lower component (b) of Area C.

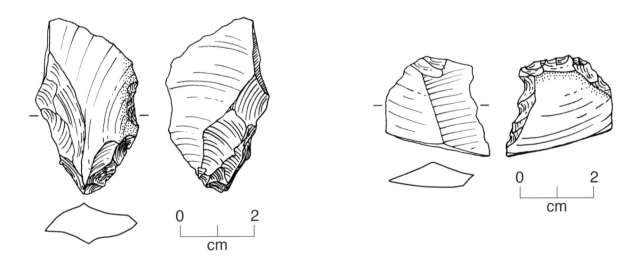

Figure 5.29. A fragment of sickle from the Jícaras phase component of Area A.

Figure 5.30. A fragment of sickle from the lower component (b) of Area C.

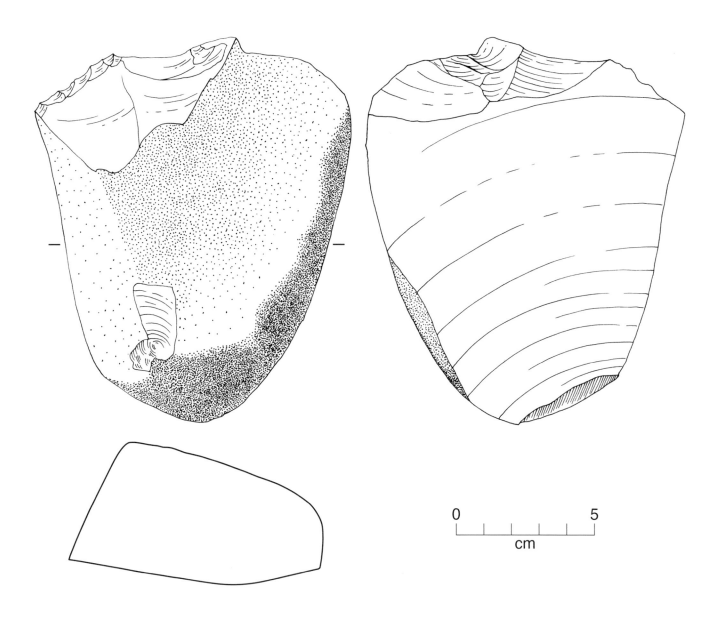

Figure 5.31. A chopper made from a cobble, found in Test Pit E22/e1.

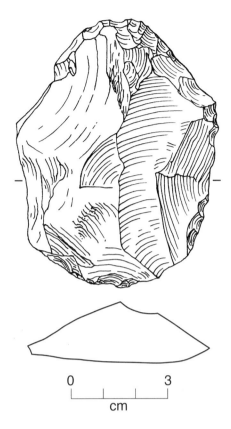

Figure 5.32. A large end scraper from the Jícaras phase component of Area A.

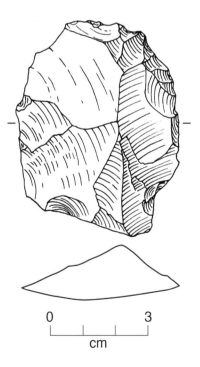

Figure 5.33. Two small end scrapers from the Jícaras phase component of Area A.

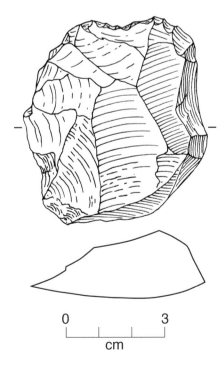

Figure 5.34. A large end scraper from the lower component (b) of Area C.

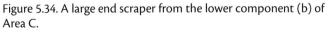

Figure 5.35. A large end scraper from the lower component (b) of Area C.

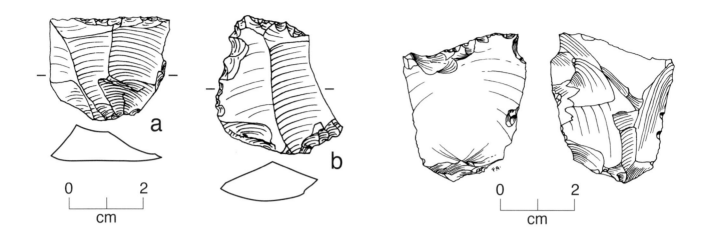

Figure 5.36. Two small end scrapers from the lower component (b) of Area C.

Figure 5.37. An end scraper from the surface (Square H3).

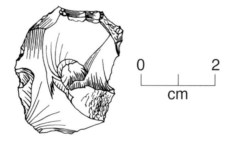

Figure 5.38. A small end scraper from the surface (Square L11).

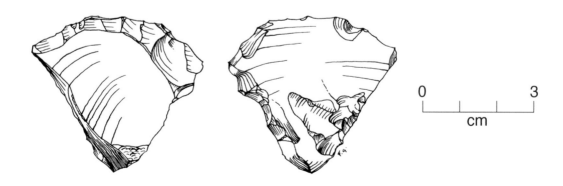

Figure 5.39. An end scraper from the surface (Square F10).

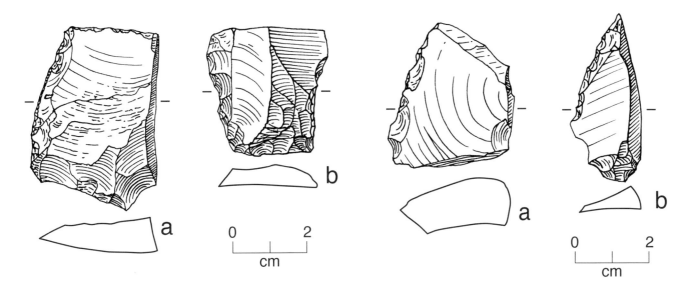

Figure 5.40. Two sidescrapers/knives from the lower component (b) of Area C.

Figure 5.41. Two sidescrapers/knives from the lower component (b) of Area C.

of the Mitla region, they were never as common in the Oaxaca Valley as they were in Tehuacán (MacNeish et al. 1967:30–43).

Sidescrapers/Knives (Figures 5.40–5.44)

These artifacts are flakes with one edge largely covered with shallow, steep, or scaling retouch. The retouched edge tends to be smooth rather than denticulate, and can be either straight or curved in outline. We suspect that these were multipurpose tools that could be used for (among other things) the skinning of animals and/or the working of hides. Sidescrapers were more common than end scrapers at all Oaxaca Archaic sites.

Steep denticulate scrapers (Figures 5.45–5.50)

Steep denticulate scrapers are heavy flakes or chunks of silicified ignimbrite or sandstone with coarse percussion retouch on one or more edges. This retouch is relatively steep to the plane of the chipping surface, and the retouched edges of the tool tend to be denticulated or notched. No effort has been made to smooth the retouched surface, as was done with both end scrapers and sidescrapers.

The largest of our steep denticulate scrapers resemble the "scraper planes" of MacNeish et al. (1967:36–39), which

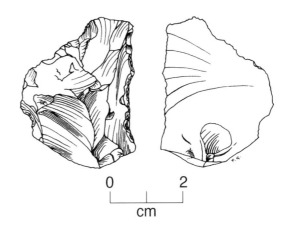

Figure 5.42. A sidescraper/knife from the surface (Square D29).

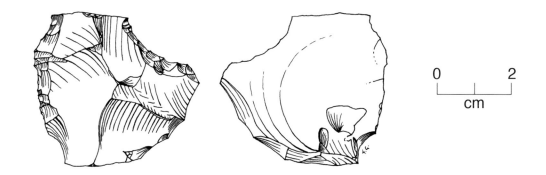

Figure 5.43. A sidescraper/knife from the surface (Square C24).

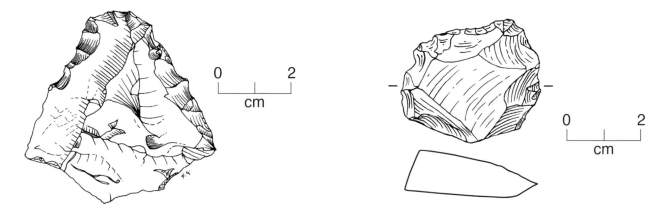

Figure 5.44. A sidescraper/knife from the surface (Square I11).

Figure 5.45. A steep denticulate scraper from the Jícaras phase component of Area A.

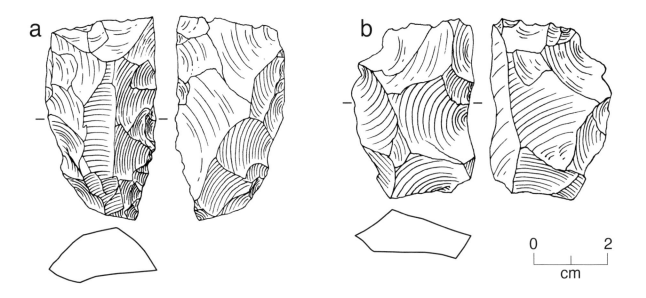

Figure 5.46. Two steep denticulate scrapers from the Jícaras phase component of Area A.

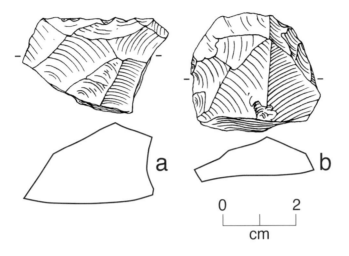

Figure 5.47. Two steep denticulate scrapers from the lower component (b) of Area C.

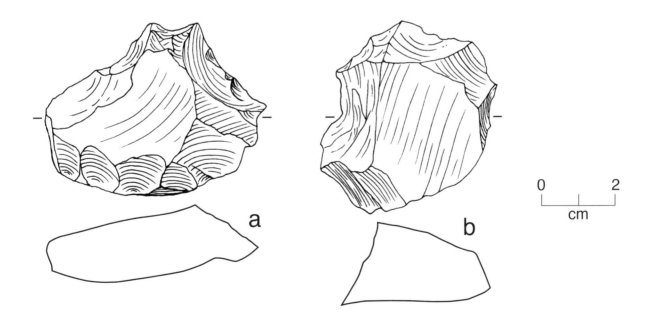

Figure 5.48. Two steep denticulate scrapers from the lower component (b) of Area C.

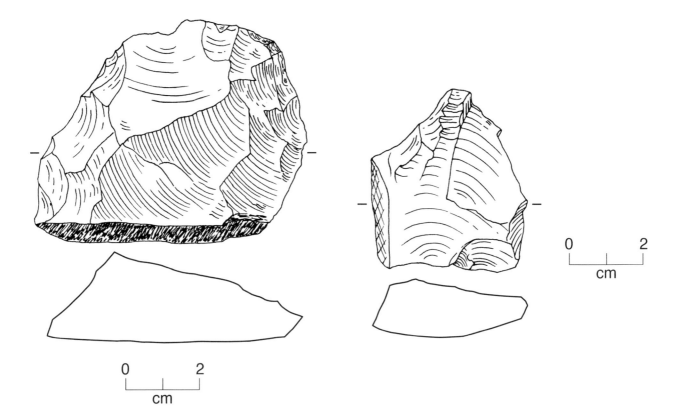

Figure 5.49. A steep denticulate scraper from the boundary between the upper and lower components of Area C.

Figure 5.50. A fragment of steep denticulate scraper from the upper component (a) of Area C.

are widely believed to have been used to shred or pulp fibrous plants such as agave and prickly pear. For what it may be worth, Gheo-Shih's steep denticulate scrapers tend to be smaller on average than those found at Cueva Blanca and Guilá Naquitz.

Tools for Slotting and Perforating

Burins (Figures 5.51–5.62)

While the frequency of burins produced by excavation at Gheo-Shih was similar to that at other Archaic sites, we found a surprising number and variety of burins on the surface. Our simplest burins had one scar from the removal of a typically J-shaped flake; in some cases, two such scars were found side by side. Our most complex, or polyhedric, burins had multiple scars where such flakes were removed from opposite ends of the tool. The large number of burins on the surface suggests that a great many cane or wooden tools were made at Gheo-Shih; unfortunately, owing to a lack of preservation, we cannot specify the nature of those tools.

Large drills, possibly hafted (Figures 5.63, 5.64)

Gheo-Shih was unique within our sample of Archaic sites in having two types of drills. The larger type, described here, had a large drill bit and a prominent stem, suggesting that it may have been hafted. We suspect that such large, hafted drills may have been used to produce biconically drilled holes in the stone ornaments described in Chapter 10. Those stone ornaments were also unique to Gheo-Shih.

Small drills/perforators (Figures 5.65–5.67)

The second type of drill found at Gheo-Shih had no stem to facilitate hafting. This was the same type of small drill used both at Cueva Blanca (Flannery and Hole 2019:87) and Formative sites like San José Mogote. At San José Mogote, it seems likely that many of these small unhafted drills were used to make shell ornaments, and Parry (1987) preferred to refer to them as "perforators." Parry was dealing with

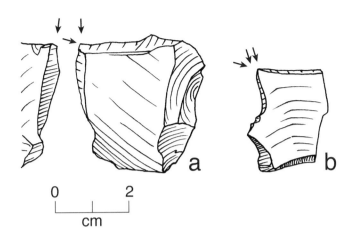

Figure 5.51. Two burins from the upper component (a) of Area C.

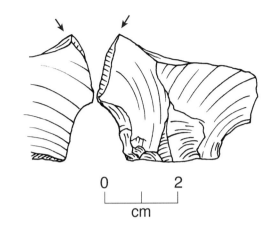

Figure 5.52. A burin from the lower component (b) of Area C.

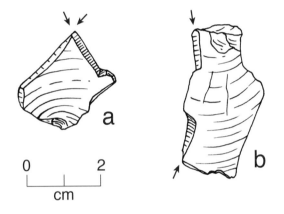

Figure 5.53. Two burins from the lower component (b) of Area C.

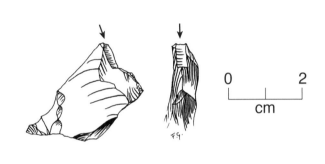

Figure 5.54. A burin from the surface (Square I14).

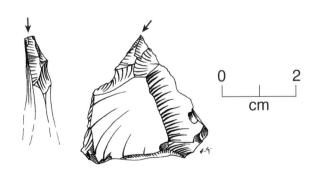

Figure 5.55. A burin from the surface (Square S5).

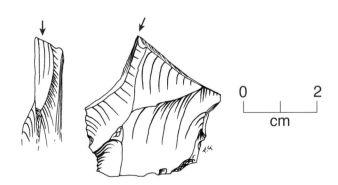

Figure 5.56. A burin from the surface (Square BB27).

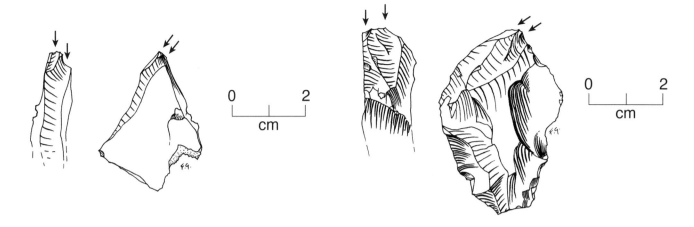

Figure 5.57. A burin from the surface (Square P2).

Figure 5.58. A burin from the surface (Square F19).

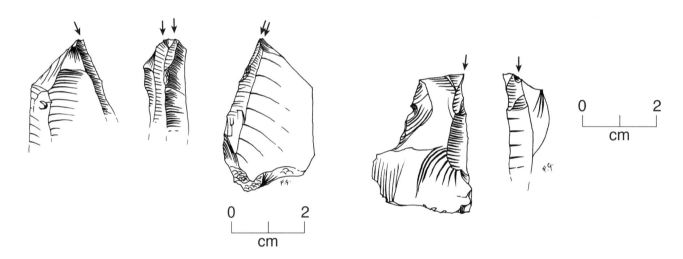

Figure 5.59. A burin from the surface (Square H14).

Figure 5.60. A burin from the surface (Square H15).

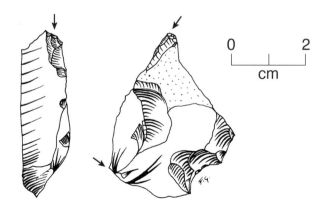

Figure 5.61. A burin from the surface (Square C18).

Chipped Stone Tools: The Typology

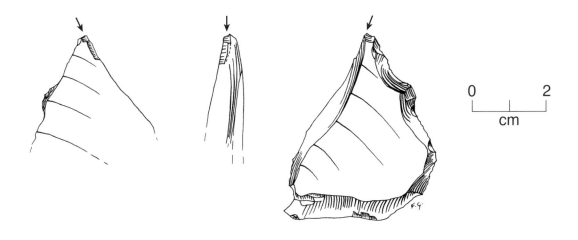

Figure 5.62. A burin from the surface (Square I24).

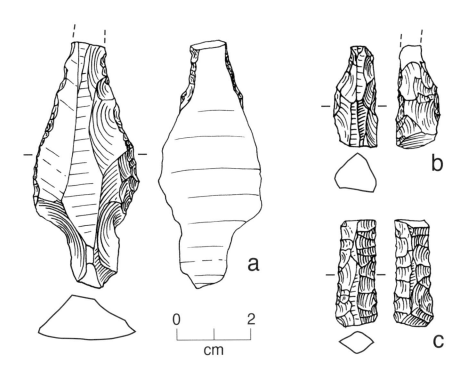

Figure 5.63. Large drills (or fragments thereof) from Gheo-Shih. *a* was found in the lower component (b) of Area C. Note that this large drill has a stem, by means of which it could have been hafted. *b* and *c* appear to be fragments of bits from large drills like the one shown in *a*. Both are from the Jícaras phase component of Area A.

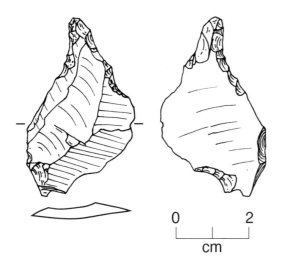

Figure 5.64. A large drill from the Jícaras phase component of Area A.

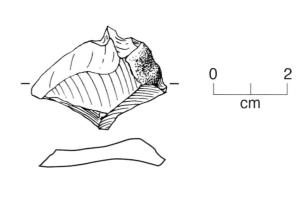

Figure 5.65. A small drill/perforator from the Jícaras phase component of Area A.

large numbers of these artifacts, and he felt that their small, nipple-like bits were not always rotated in the manner of a drill.

Bifaces

Oaxaca's Archaic bifaces displayed a wide variety of forms—from well-made spear and atlatl points, to the roughouts or preforms for those points, to simpler bifaces that could be used as cutting tools. As in previous studies (Flannery and Hole 2019), we have separated projectile points into their own category. The other bifaces form a continuum from relatively crude to relatively well made; we have divided this continuum into three varieties, labeled A, B, and C.

Bifaces, Variety A (Figures 5.68–5.75)

Variety A includes our best-made examples of bifaces—for example, the ones we have called "Martínez bifaces" (Flannery and Hole 2019: Figs. 5.45–5.46). Martínez bifaces were made on flakes thinned with careful bifacial retouch on the planar surfaces and were often almond-shaped in outline. We suspect that many Variety A bifaces were the preforms from which projectile points were to be made, although their smooth, straight edges could have been used for a variety of tasks. Their name is a reference to the Martínez Rockshelter, a Late Archaic site that produced some of our best examples (Flannery and Spores 2003).

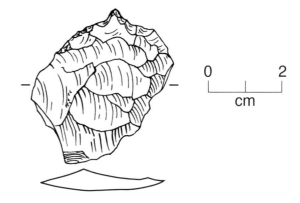

Figure 5.66. A small drill/perforator from the lower component (b) of Area C.

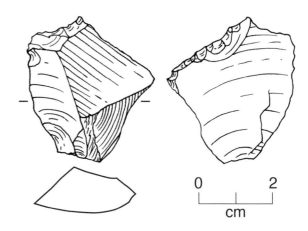

Figure 5.67. A small drill/perforator from the upper component (a) of Area C.

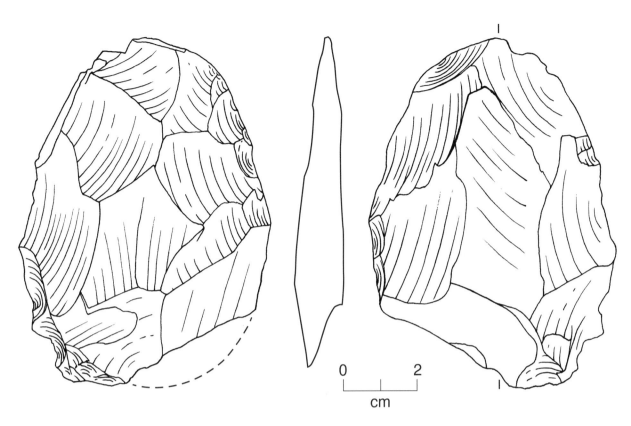

Figure 5.68. A damaged Variety A biface from the surface of Gheo-Shih. It was piece-plotted in Square L30, 210 cm from the east border and 180 cm from the south border.

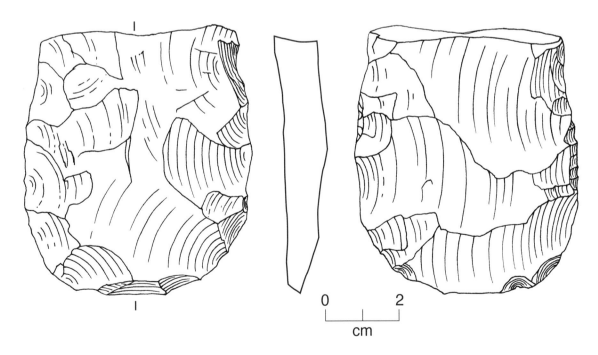

Figure 5.69. A broken Variety A biface from the surface. It was piece-plotted in Square I23, 85 cm from the east border and 200 cm from the south border.

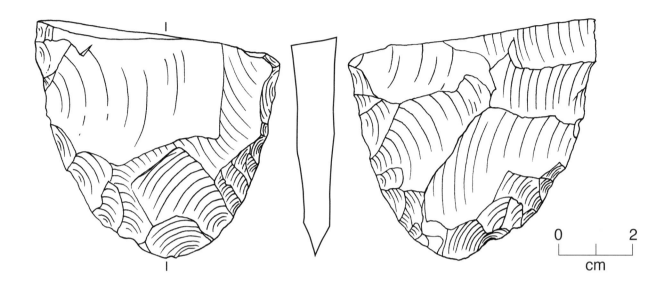

Figure 5.70. A broken Variety A biface from the surface. It was piece-plotted in Square F10, 252 cm from the west border and 202 cm from the north border.

Bifaces, Variety B (Figures 5.76–5.81)

This variety consists largely of flakes with good bifacial chipping, mostly confined to the edges, leaving the flake relatively thick compared to Variety A. The bases are usually unfinished when present and show either a striking platform or a clean break. Variety B bifaces tend to have an ogival silhouette.

Bifaces, Variety C (Figures 5.82–5.90)

Variety C consists of the crudest and most asymmetrical of our bifaces. These tools are generally thick flakes with one or more edges modified by coarse bifacial retouch. The bodies of the flakes have not been thinned and their outlines show a range of shapes, often irregularly round or oval. None of our Variety C bifaces would have made good preforms for projectile points; it is likely that they were crude tools in their own right.

Projectile points

Gheo-Shih provided us with our largest sample of Archaic projectile points. All were bifacially chipped, relatively large points, intended either for an atlatl dart or a thrusting spear. They could be made of chert, chalcedony, silicified volcanic tuff, or silicified sedimentary rock.

Because of their relatively high level of stylistic information, and its relevance to the establishment of a sequence of chronological phases for the Oaxaca Archaic, we have devoted Chapter 7 to these bifacial artifacts.

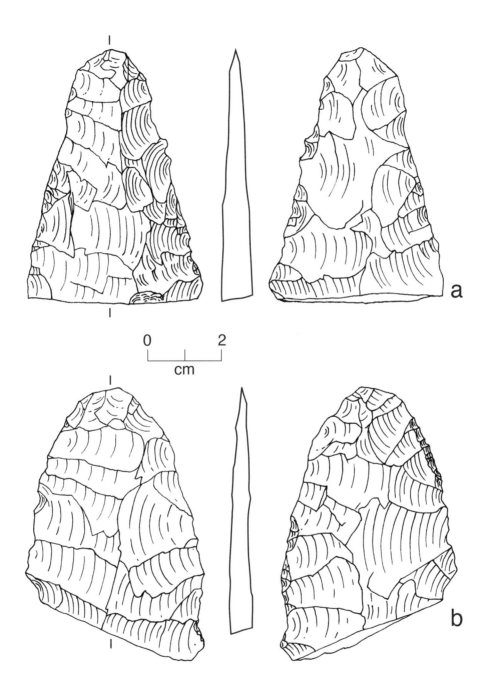

Figure 5.71. The tapered ends of two Variety A bifaces from the surface. *a* was piece-plotted in Square O5, 15 cm from the west border and 30 cm from the north border. *b* was found in Square K30.

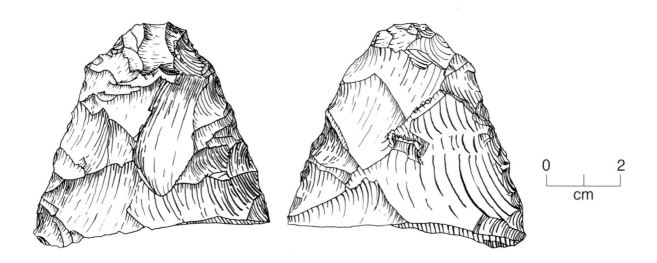

Figure 5.72. The tapered end of a Variety A biface, found on the surface in Square I8.

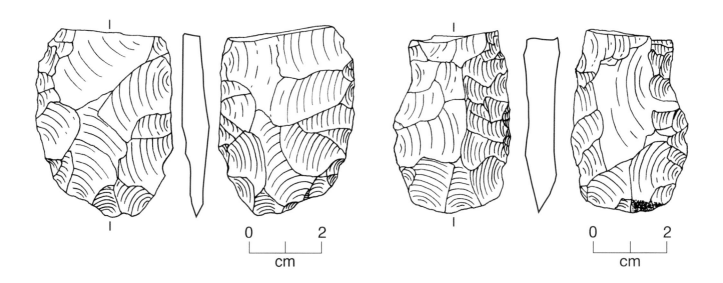

Figure 5.73. A damaged Variety A biface from the surface. It was piece-plotted in Square BB30, 165 cm from the west border and 300 cm from the north border.

Figure 5.74. A damaged Variety A biface from the upper component (a) of Area C.

Chipped Stone Tools: The Typology

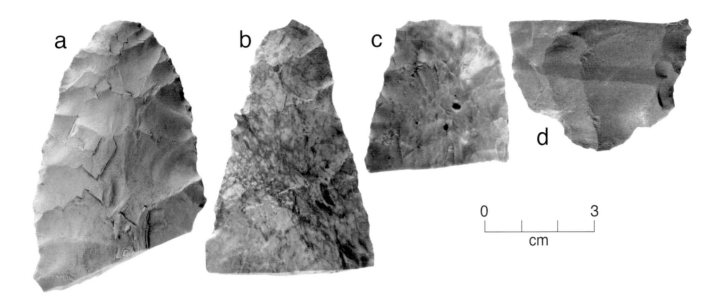

Figure 5.75. Fragments of Variety A bifaces, recovered from the surface of Gheo-Shih. *a* was found in Square K30; *b*, in Square O5; *c*, in Square F5; *d*, in Square S8.

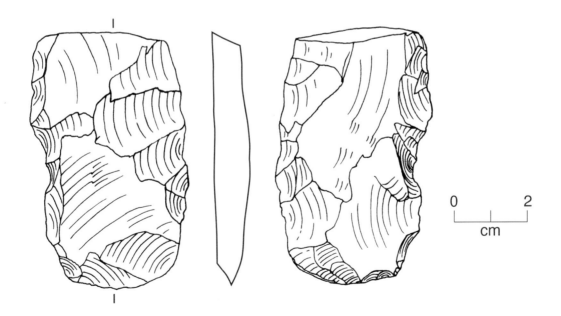

Figure 5.76. A damaged Variety B biface, found on the surface some 100 m south of the site of Gheo-Shih.

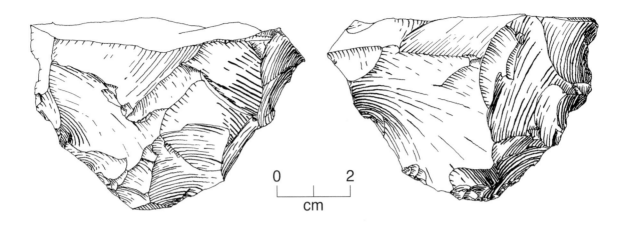

Figure 5.77. The base of a broken Variety B biface, found on the surface of Gheo-Shih (Square K30).

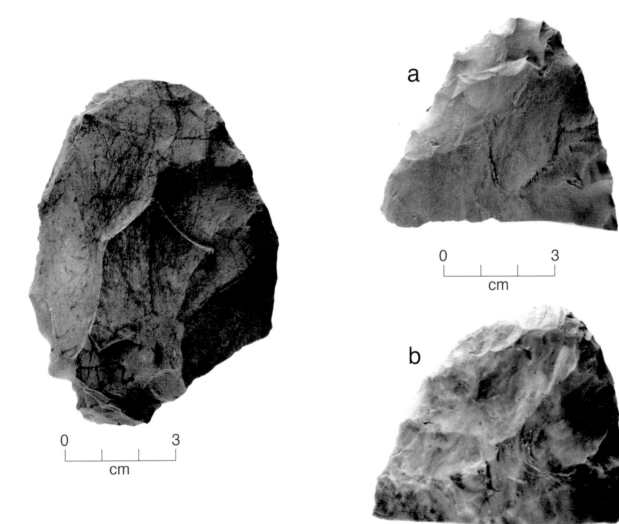

Figure 5.78. A damaged Variety B biface recovered from the surface (Square L30).

Figure 5.79. Two fragments of Variety B bifaces recovered from the surface of Gheo-Shih. *a* was found in Square I8; *b* was found in Square F10.

Figure 5.81. A broken Variety B biface from the lower component (b) of Area C.

Figure 5.80. Two fragments of Variety B bifaces from the upper component (a) of Area C.

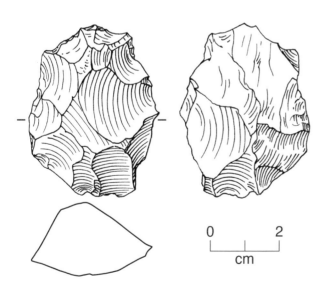

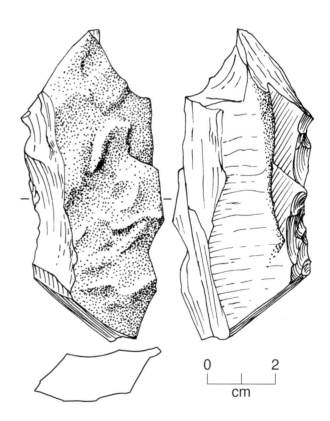

Figure 5.82. A small Variety C biface from the Jícaras phase component of Area A.

Figure 5.83. A broken Variety C biface from the Jícaras phase component of Area A.

Figure 5.84. Variety C bifaces from the Jícaras phase component of Area A.

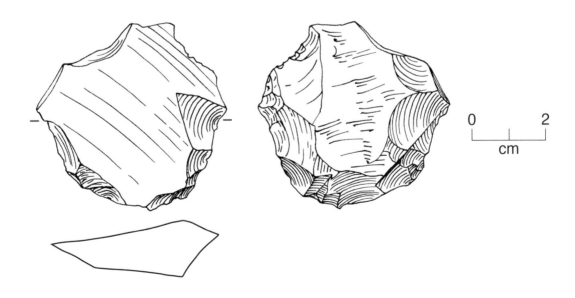

Figure 5.85. A Variety C biface from the upper component (a) of Area C.

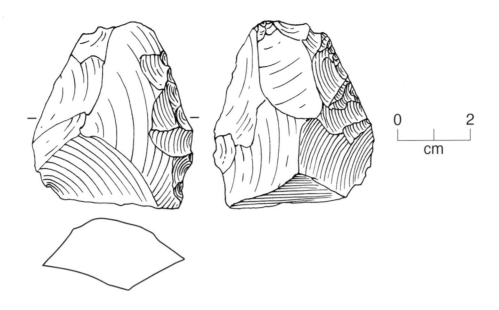

Figure 5.86. A damaged Variety C biface from the lower component (b) of Area C.

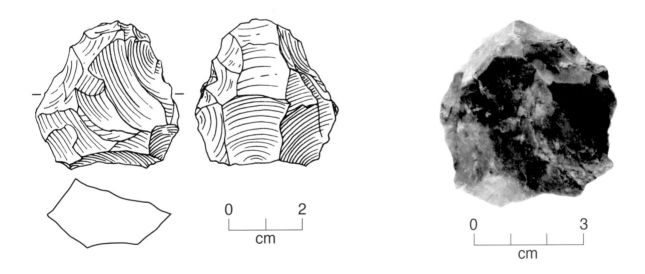

Figure 5.87. A damaged Variety C biface from the lower component (b) of Area C.

Figure 5.88. A small Variety C biface from the upper component (a) of Area C.

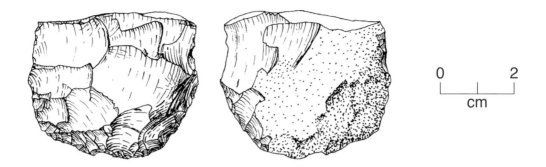

Figure 5.89. A broken Variety C biface from the surface of Gheo-Shih (Square BB30).

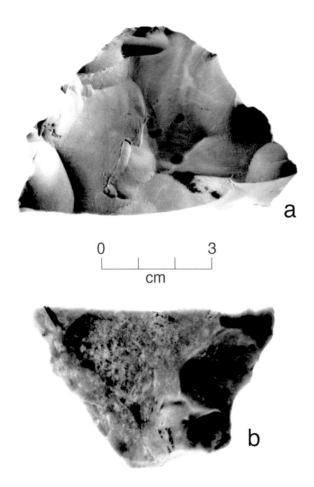

Figure 5.90. Fragments of Variety C bifaces recovered from the surface. *a* was found in Square K30; *b* was found in Square A16.

Chapter 6

Chipped Stone Tools: The Horizontal Distribution

In Chapter 5 we provided definitions for all of the Archaic chipped stone tool types recognized at Gheo-Shih. In this chapter we take on an equally important task: establishing the vertical (stratigraphic) location of each tool type and its horizontal distribution within each stratigraphic level. We searched for several types of information, including (1) evidence of tool clusters that may represent activity areas, and (2) indications that certain activities might have been restricted to one stratigraphic level or to one part of the site. Note that one group of chipped stone tools—projectile points—is not included in this chapter, since the points will be covered in detail in Chapters 7 and 8.

Area A

The most significant stratigraphic distinction in Area A was between the basal level—which dated to the late Naquitz phase and contained the important ritual feature discussed in Chapter 4—and the overlying Jícaras phase component. Since the late Naquitz phase feature appeared to have been swept clean of artifacts, the basal level of Area A contributed little information in terms of tool distribution. A concentration of pebbles and debitage northeast of the feature may indicate the presence of an ephemeral structure, but the lack of retouched tools was notable.

The overlying Jícaras phase component was a different story. We recovered some 581 chipped stone tools from this component; in addition, there were 11,754 pieces of debitage. For what it is worth, the three most numerous tool categories were core fragments, notched flakes, and steep denticulate scrapers. On the other hand, the Jícaras phase component of Area A produced no choppers, no Variety A bifaces, and no retouched blades.

Let us now look at the distribution of some significant tool types by plotting their location on the grid of 1 x 1 m squares from Area A. We decided not to plot every type—for example, we have plotted all the flake cores but not the fragments thereof, which were so numerous and widespread as to defy patterning. We also have not plotted those types whose frequency was so low that they seemed unlikely to reveal any clustering.

We begin with the 32 hammerstones (Figure 6.1) and 64 flake cores (Figure 6.2) from the Jícaras phase component. Since we assume that some hammerstones were used to strike flakes off cores, we were naturally interested to see whether these two potentially associated tool types had been discarded in the same locations.

We immediately notice a semicircle of seven hammerstones, running from square G25/e3 to square G27/a3; a roughly comparable semicircle runs from H26/c1 to G28/c3. This makes us wonder if those two semicircles might represent the outer limits of a chert knapping area, centered on the southern half of Square G26 and the northern half of Square G27.

If we turn to the distribution of flake cores, we note a rough semicircle of 11–14 cores running from square G25/d3 to square G27/a4. While the overlap between this semicircle of cores and our second semicircle of hammerstones is not perfect, it is close enough to attract our attention.

In other parts of the grid, however, these two tool types show less overlap. For example, some 15 cores were discarded in 5 x 5 m Square E26, but that square yielded only one hammerstone. Thus that square, in the northwest quadrant of Area A, is not a plausible candidate for a knapping area. This fact should remind us that hammerstones were probably used for a wide variety of tasks, rather than being limited to striking flakes from cores.

Let us turn now to the 11,754 pieces of debitage from the Jícaras phase component (Figure 6.3). Our first impression is that debitage was everywhere. Our second impression is that any attempt to draw meaningful density contours of debitage would likely be futile. The counts per 1 x 1 m square vary from zero to 116, and appear random rather than showing systematic peaks and valleys.

This situation is very different from that encountered in our Archaic cave sites. At both Guilá Naquitz and Cueva Blanca, Spencer and Flannery (2009, 2019) were able to produce density contours of waste flakes for a number of cave living floors. The fact that we cannot do so for Area A of Gheo-Shih raises an interesting possibility. It may be that family microband camps were of such short duration that their activity areas were still relatively intact when the occupants left the cave. Large macroband camps, on the other hand, were of longer duration. It is possible that activities at macroband camps went on so long that we are sometimes left with a palimpsest of superimposed activity areas. In such a palimpsest, it would be much more difficult to produce meaningful density contours.

Next, let us look at the distribution of utilized flakes (Figure 6.4) and notched flakes (Figure 6.5). Since both of these tool types owe a great deal of their final form to use

Table 6.1. Chipped stone tools from Jícaras phase levels in Area A.

Hammerstones	32
Flake cores	64
Core fragments	172
Utilized flakes	42
Notched flakes	96
Flakes with bulbar end retouch	—
Crude blades, plain	21
Crude blades, retouched	—
Flakes with sheen	2
Sickles	3
Choppers	—
End scrapers	10
Sidescrapers/knives	17
Steep denticulate scrapers	78
Burins	19
Drills	8
Bifaces, Variety A	—
Bifaces, Variety B	4
Bifaces, Variety C	10
Projectile points	3
Total	**581**

wear, we would not have been surprised to find that their distributions were similar; however, they are not. In the first place, more than twice as many notched flakes as utilized flakes were discarded in the Jícaras phase component of Area A. In addition, more than half of the 96 notched flakes were recovered from the east half of Area A, while more than half of the 42 utilized flakes were recovered from the west half. Whatever tasks notched flakes may have been used for, it appears that those tasks were carried out over a wide area of the Jícaras phase component.

One aspect of the utilized flake distribution (Figure 6.4) may be worth mentioning. We believe that we can detect an oval scatter of 11–18 utilized flakes in the northeast quadrant of Area A. This oval loosely overlaps with the semicircles of hammerstones and flake cores mentioned earlier in this chapter. It reinforces our suspicion that there may have been an activity area in the northeast quadrant, one where someone used hammerstones to strike flakes off cores, then utilized some of the flakes for light cutting tasks.

Chipped Stone Tools: The Horizontal Distribution

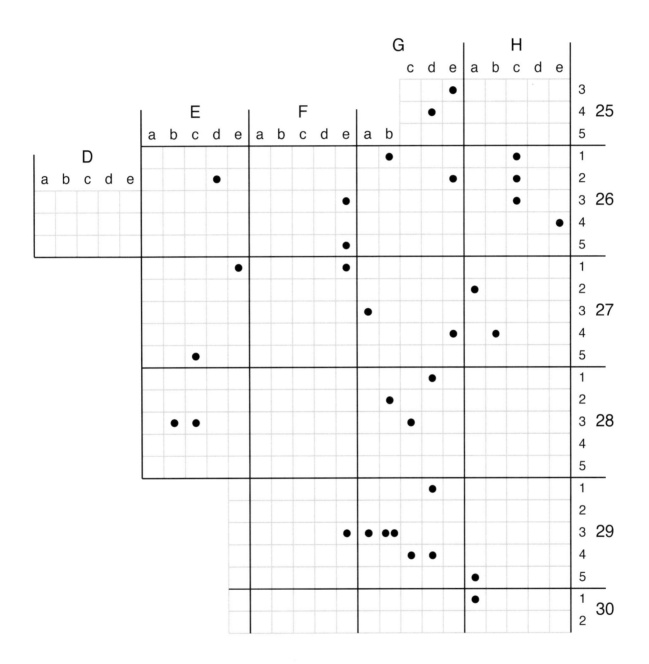

Figure 6.1. The distribution of hammerstones throughout the Jícaras phase component of Area A. In this and subsequent figures, north is at the top of the grid.

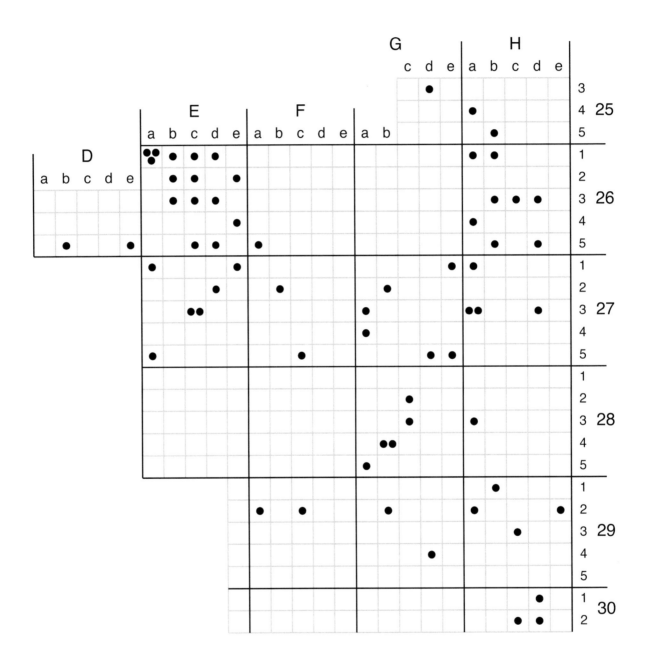

Figure 6.2. The distribution of flake cores throughout the Jícaras phase component of Area A.

Chipped Stone Tools: The Horizontal Distribution

Row	D-a	D-b	D-c	D-d	D-e	E-a	E-b	E-c	E-d	E-e	F-a	F-b	F-c	F-d	F-e	G-a	G-b	G-c	G-d	G-e	H-a	H-b	H-c	H-d	H-e
25-3																		48	40	40	34	42	27	48	30
25-4																		30	51	41	35	33	16	21	20
25-5																		70	33	43	21	29	18	17	28
26-1						54	67	68	58	21	28	116	24	31	64	47	55	26	28	33	12	44	38	18	17
26-2						38	54	33	31	41	81	43	29	39	48	40	23	26	35	35	24	34	66	31	52
26-3	21	10	11	19	39	33	43	34	22	36	32	59	19	18	19	16	38	25	12	14	33	58	47	15	32
26-4	12	16	16	26	36	34	39	41	30	46	36	60	35	41	39	34	32	27	7	20	34	54	42	17	12
26-5	10	14	10	9	41	21	33	32	29	13	37	43	59	70	54	28	26	12	45	13	29	41	29	22	10
27-1						11	12	23	16	45	21	29	35	53	22	53	33	29	22	22	54	36	27	22	20
27-2						14	25	28	23	15	13	49	27	36	33	40	10	24	28	32	39	22	29	20	27
27-3						15	31	24	33	40	20	24	28	25	19	40	37	34	32	28	76	31	35	31	35
27-4						9	13	22	15	29	28	32	38	21	33	19	22	38	22	28	52	19	47	9	24
27-5						12	14	21	13	20	17	47	40	31	20	23	29	22	22	21	21	39	27	33	25
28-1						26	33	25	12	24	21	20	47	32	28	25	16	25	26	29	17	6	11	11	38
28-2						20	23	16	23	26	28	28	27	36	14	25	17	28	52	28	14	7	18	6	9
28-3						12	23	12	15	26	36	27	12	15	11	24	11	13	15	11	9	13	23	14	13
28-4						24	3	8	16	28	20	9	37	32	34	27	30	14	12	22	8	7	7	15	35
28-5						53	21	10	8	15	14	16	16	17	26	17	56	36	41	37	17	9	1	13	16
29-1										4	34	48	17	22	15	13	29	21	33	35	30	1	5	18	23
29-2										1	11	27	29	29	22	30	19	15	21	12	6	12	8	16	21
29-3										4	15	26	23	30	38	49	39	40	19	15	10	7	7	10	21
29-4										0	11	13	21	30	33	37	26	27	37	18	18	10	16	12	11
29-5										7	7	22	6	15	17	22	26	25	23	49	18	22	33	16	19
30-1										6	6	2	12	5	8	14	11	15	38	26	18	41	49	53	32
30-2										3	3	6	9	10	14	3	8	8	16	11	17	42	28	40	37

Figure 6.3. The distribution of debitage throughout the Jícaras phase component of Area A, by 1 x 1 m square.

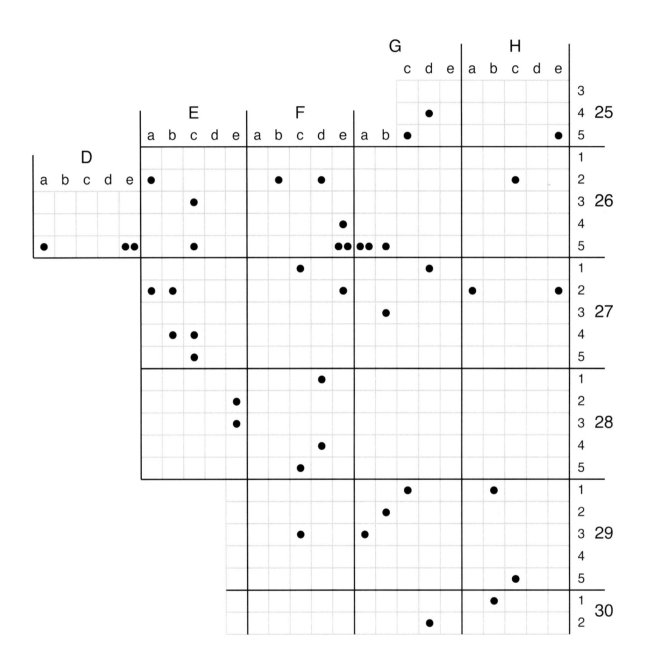

Figure 6.4. The distribution of utilized flakes throughout the Jícaras phase component of Area A.

Chipped Stone Tools: The Horizontal Distribution

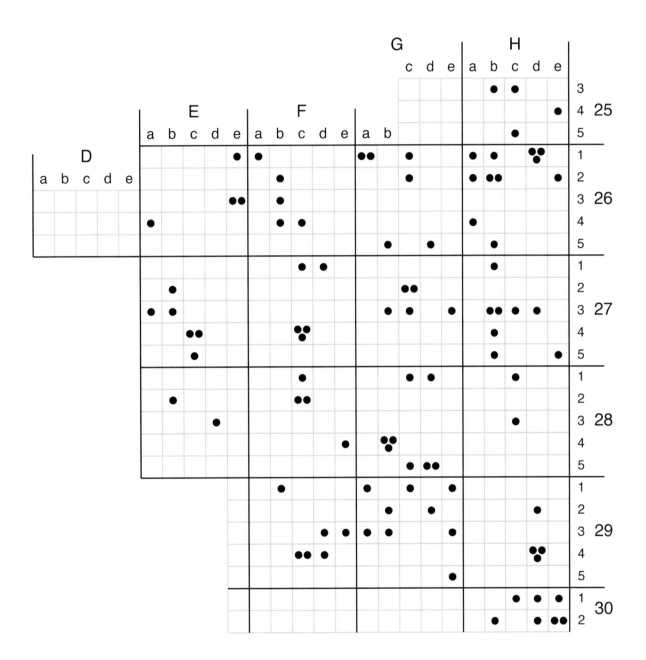

Figure 6.5. The distribution of notched flakes throughout the Jícaras phase component of Area A.

Let us turn now to unretouched crude blades (Figure 6.6). We see that more than half of the 21 blades were discarded in the eastern half of Area A, and six to eight of these were found in the southeast quadrant. However, we are not convinced that we can detect a believable cluster of unretouched blades.

Figure 6.7 shows the distribution of our 10 end scrapers. Eight of these could be seen as forming a circle with Square G28 at its center. It is, to be sure, a very large circle, at least 12 m in diameter. However, we cannot rule out the possibility that we are seeing eight end scrapers that were tossed to the margins of an activity area (Binford 1978).

Significantly, sidescrapers/knives do not show a similar distribution (Figure 6.8). Our 17 examples of this tool type were spread widely over Area A; the only grouping that catches our eye is a lozenge-shaped area, centered on Square G26 and consisting of nine sidescrapers/knives. What this tells us is that sidescrapers and end scrapers were not likely to be discarded together, and presumably were used for different tasks.

We recovered some 78 steep denticulate scrapers from the Jícaras phase component of Area A (Figure 6.9). They were widely distributed, with more than half of them discarded in the northeastern part of the excavation; many 5 x 5 m squares produced 8–10 examples. The best we can say is that the occupants of Area A engaged in a lot of coarse scraping or "scraper plane" activity.

Two of the most interesting distributions were those of burins (Figure 6.10) and drills (Figure 6.11). We immediately note (1) six burins forming a possible semicircle near the southern limits of our excavation, and (2) a scatter of nine burins in the center of Area A. If we turn next to the distribution of our eight drills (Figure 6.11), we immediately notice four drills forming a possible semicircle near the southern limits of the excavation. We then notice a scatter of three drills in the center of Area A, occupying roughly the same area as the previously mentioned scatter of nine burins. The distributions in Figures 6.10 and 6.11, therefore, suggest that burins and drills tended to be discarded in the same areas. This raises the possibility that certain types of artifact production—involving both of these so-called "tools used to make other tools"—were carried out in Area A of Gheo-Shih.

Finally, we come to bifaces of Varieties B and C. The distributions of Variety B (Figure 6.12) and Variety C (Figure 6.13) do not look similar at all. This gives us some confidence that our separation of these two varieties of bifaces is defensible on functional grounds. Although our varieties could be seen as subjective distinctions made within a continuum of bifaces, Figures 6.12 and 6.13 do not suggest that Varieties B and C were used interchangeably or discarded together.

Area C: The Lower Component (b)

We turn next to Area C, where two Jícaras phase components have been distinguished. We will consider them in chronological order, beginning with b, the lower and earlier of the two components.

We recovered 340 chipped stone tools and 3464 pieces of debitage from component b of Area C. We chose 17 categories of chipped stone for distributional analysis; most were chosen because of their relatively high numbers, although some of the less numerous tools were added owing to their potential significance.

Table 6.2. Chipped stone tools from the lower component (b) of Area C.

Hammerstones	12
Flake cores	31
Core fragments	67
Utilized flakes	33
Notched flakes	76
Flakes with bulbar end retouch	3
Crude blades, plain	15
Crude blades, retouched	6
Flakes with sheen	3
Sickles	2
Choppers	—
End scrapers	5
Sidescrapers/knives	12
Steep denticulate scrapers	43
Burins	7
Drills	3
Bifaces, Variety A	3
Bifaces, Variety B	8
Bifaces, Variety C	5
Projectile points	6
Total	**342**

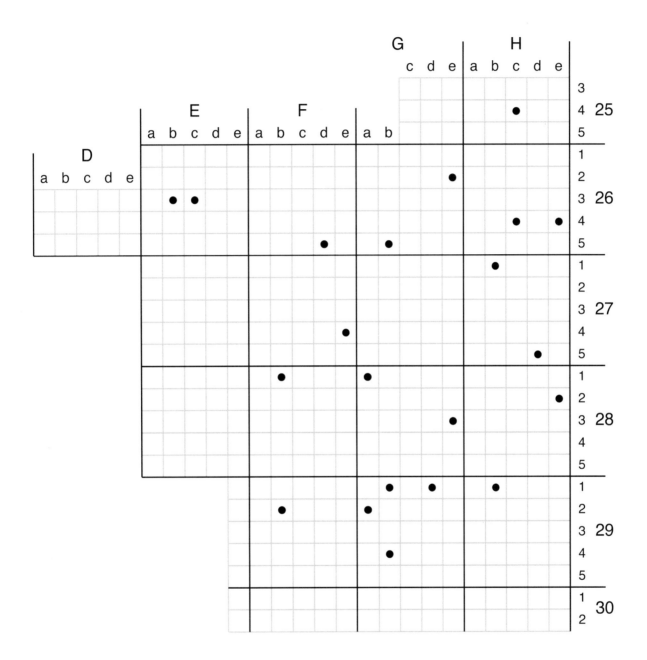

Figure 6.6. The distribution of crude blades (plain) throughout the Jícaras phase component of Area A.

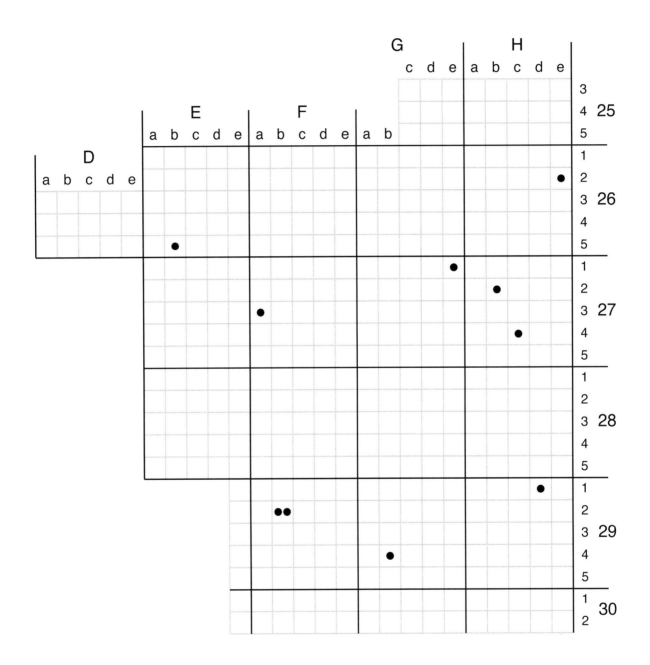

Figure 6.7. The distribution of end scrapers throughout the Jícaras phase component of Area A.

Chipped Stone Tools: The Horizontal Distribution

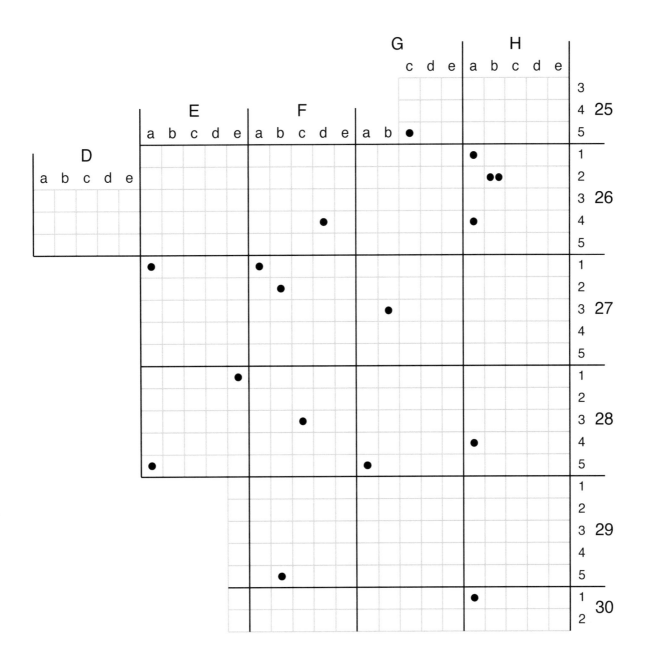

Figure 6.8. The distribution of sidescrapers/knives throughout the Jícaras phase component of Area A.

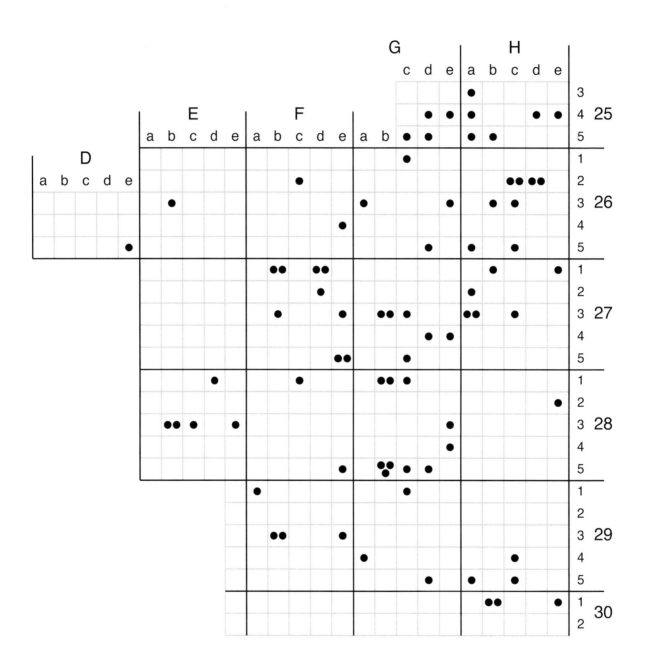

Figure 6.9. The distribution of steep denticulate scrapers throughout the Jícaras phase component of Area A.

Chipped Stone Tools: The Horizontal Distribution

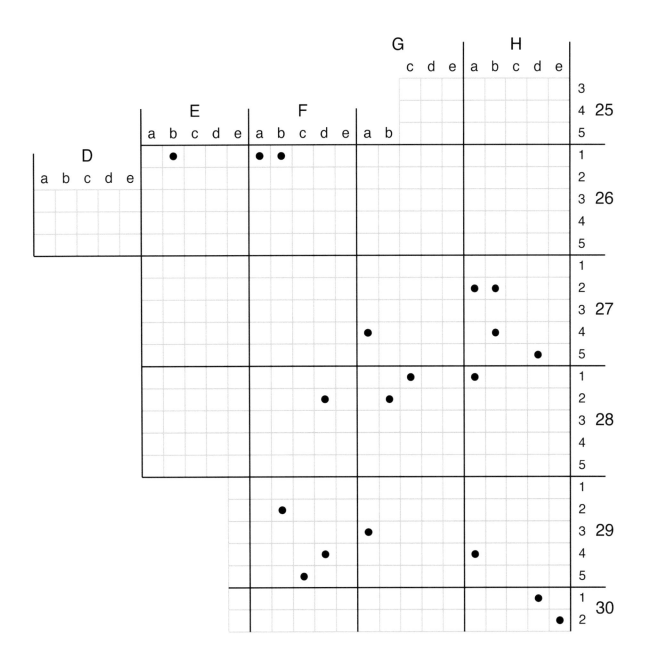

Figure 6.10. The distribution of burins throughout the Jícaras phase component of Area A.

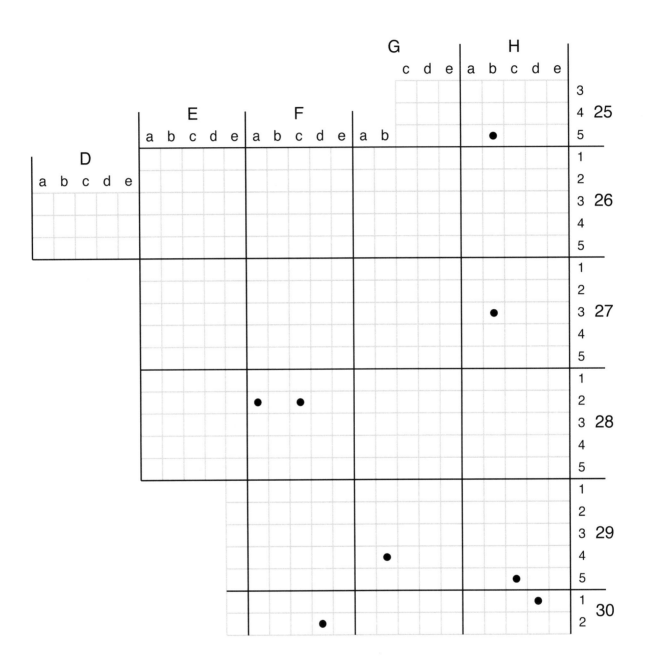

Figure 6.11. The distribution of drills throughout the Jícaras phase component of Area A.

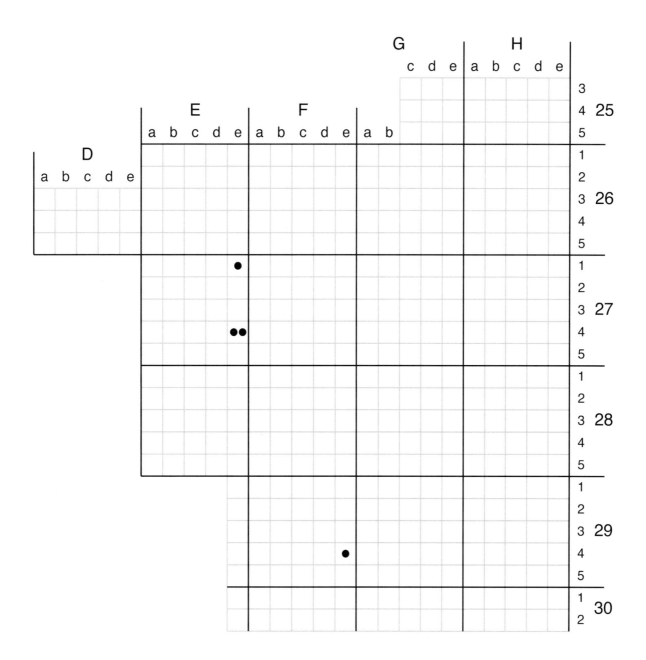

Figure 6.12. The distribution of Variety B bifaces throughout the Jícaras phase component of Area A.

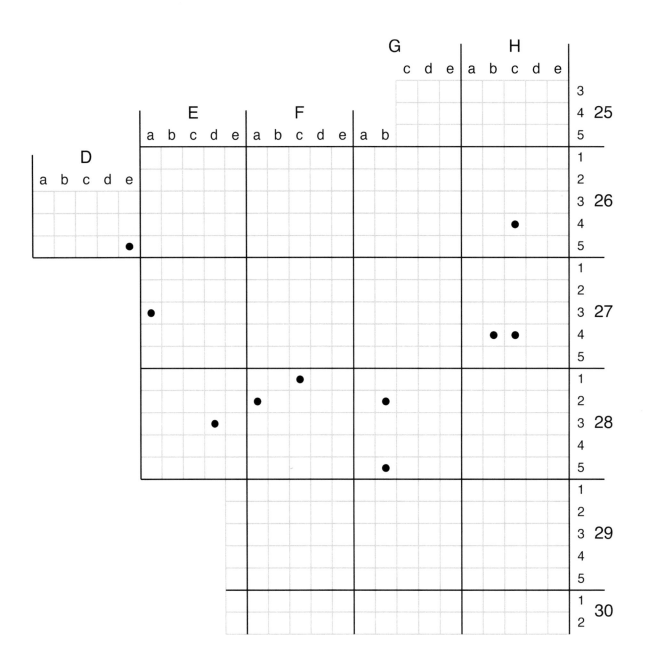

Figure 6.13. The distribution of Variety C bifaces throughout the Jícaras phase component of Area A.

Hammerstones (Figure 6.14). Nine of the 12 hammerstones from component b were found in the northwest half of Area C, suggesting that Squares D14 and D15 might have fallen within an area where hammering activities were carried out.

Flake cores (Figure 6.15). Some 20 of the 31 flake cores from component b were found in Squares E14, E15, and E16, in the eastern portion of Area A. The contrast between Figures 6.14 and 6.15 suggests that hammerstones and cores were not discarded together. Recall that in our analysis of Area A, we concluded that hammerstones were likely used for a greater variety of tasks than simply flint knapping.

Debitage (Figure 6.16). Some 3464 pieces of debitage were recovered from component b of Area C. No convincing concentrations were observed, although it does appear that 5 × 5 m Squares E14, E15, and E16, which produced the bulk of the flake cores, also had the highest debitage counts.

Utilized flakes (Figure 6.17). The 33 utilized flakes from component b did appear to form a few tentative clusters, the most striking of which was a group of eight from the eastern half of Square E14. Nine more came from Square E15, and four from the center of Square D14. We are not sure whether the eight from Square D15 represent two clusters or one. At any rate, we see some evidence that there may have been locations in component b where some kind of activity produced multiple utilized flakes; two of those locations were in Squares E14 and E15, where there were also numerous flake cores. Recall that in the Jícaras phase component of Area A, there was a similar relationship between cores and utilized flakes.

Notched flakes (Figure 6.18). We recovered some 76 notched flakes from component b. These tools were so widely distributed throughout Area C that it is difficult to point to specific clusters. Recall that the situation in Area A was similar.

Flakes with bulbar end retouch (Figure 6.19). There were only three of these artifacts in component b, and all were found near the center of Square E15. While we cannot assign a function to this tool type, we note that it was both (1) restricted to component b and (2) relatively clustered. No examples of this rare tool type were found elsewhere at Gheo-Shih.

Crude blades, plain (Figure 6.20). All but two of the 15 crude blades from component b occurred in a semicircular scatter in the northern part of Area C. Squares D14 and D15 had the largest number.

Crude blades, retouched (Figure 6.21). We recovered only six retouched blades from component b. What is striking about their distribution is how different it appears from that of the unretouched blades. Four of the retouched blades occur in the extreme south of Area C (Squares D16 and E16); only one of our unretouched blades was found in this location.

End scrapers (Figure 6.22). We recovered only five end scrapers from component b. All were found in the northern part of Area C (Squares C14–E14), well within the semicircular distribution of plain blades. In other words, there are hints of an activity area involving both cutting and scraping, which was not the case in Area A.

Sidescrapers/knives (Figure 6.23). We recovered 12 sidescrapers/knives from component b. All occurred in the southern half of Area C (D15–D16, E15–E16), well away from the semicircular scatter of plain blades and end scrapers. This distribution strengthens our impression that end scrapers and sidescrapers/knives were used for different tasks and discarded in different areas.

Steep denticulate scrapers (Figure 6.24). We recovered 44 steep denticulate scrapers from component b. This tool type was so numerous and widely distributed that we find it difficult to identify convincing clusters.

Burins (Figure 6.25). Seven burins were recovered from component b. We found six of these in the northeast quadrant; 5 × 5 m Square E14 alone produced four burins. While we cannot specify the task for which burins were used, we find this clustering intriguing.

Drills (Figure 6.26). We found four drills in component b. This was a small number, and the distribution of drills did not suggest a close association with any other tool type; that fact was disappointing, given the possible association of burins and drills in Area A. In Chapter 10, we suggest that the largest of our drills may have been used to make the biconically drilled stone discs found in component b.

Bifaces, Variety A (Figure 6.27). Three Variety A bifaces were recovered from component b. While all three were found in the southern portion of Area C, there was no convincing evidence of clustering. Recall that Area A produced no examples of Variety A bifaces, which were relatively rare in the components we excavated.

Bifaces, Variety B (Figure 6.28). The eight Variety B bifaces from component b appear to have been discarded in two scatters. One scatter lay in the northeast (mainly in Square E14), while the other lay in the south (mainly in Square D16). Their distribution is strikingly different from that of the Variety A bifaces, suggesting that the two varieties were not interchangeable.

Bifaces, Variety C (Figure 6.29). Only five Variety C bifaces were recovered from component b. Their distribution does not show any clustering, nor does it closely resemble the distributions of Varieties A or B. This fact makes our separation of the three varieties reasonable.

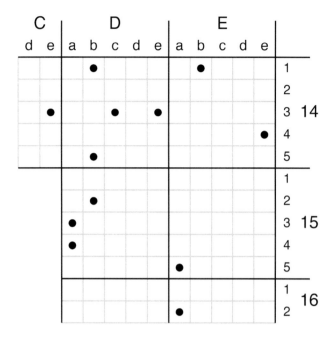

Figure 6.14. The distribution of hammerstones throughout the lower component (b) of Area C.

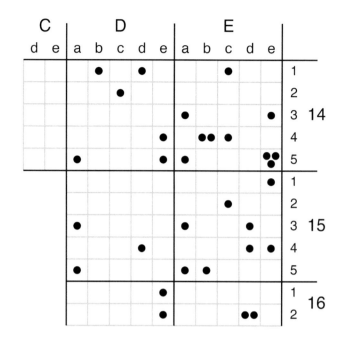

Figure 6.15. The distribution of flake cores throughout the lower component (b) of Area C.

	C		D					E				
d	e	a	b	c	d	e	a	b	c	d	e	
10	16	8	20	12	27	25	17	15	18	0	21	1
2	9	55	18	1	15	21	0	14	11	0	58	2
5	30	33	31	19	24	34	16	0	40	26	26	3	14
17	54	21	15	14	29	28	26	23	60	27	33	4
23	21	46	27	16	20	25	25	34	14	17	20	5
		20	41	54	53	0	35	23	41	54	29	1
		31	0	21	53	0	24	43	0	81	55	2
		30	13	34	21	19	8	51	6	25	78	3	15
		28	30	32	25	35	4	34	62	10	60	4
		39	27	32	27	59	53	62	30	30	28	5
		32	25	16	17	20	2	10	11	35	54	1	16
		22	35	4	43	20	4	50	53	33	16	2

Figure 6.16. The distribution of debitage throughout the lower component (b) of Area C, by 1 x 1 m square.

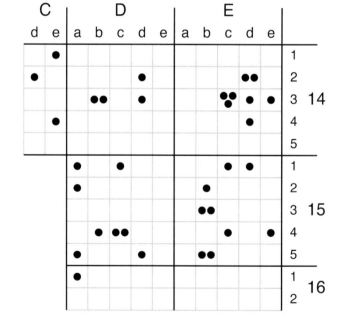

Figure 6.17. The distribution of utilized flakes throughout the lower component (b) of Area C.

Chipped Stone Tools: The Horizontal Distribution

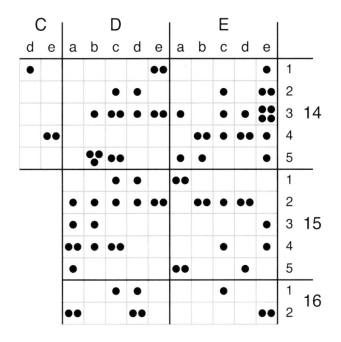

Figure 6.18. The distribution of notched flakes throughout the lower component (b) of Area C.

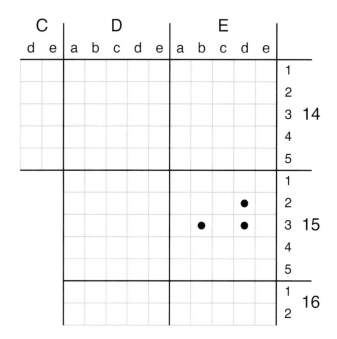

Figure 6.19. The distribution of flakes with bulbar end retouch throughout the lower component (b) of Area C.

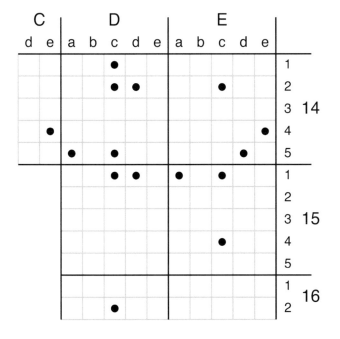

Figure 6.20. The distribution of crude blades (plain) throughout the lower component (b) of Area C.

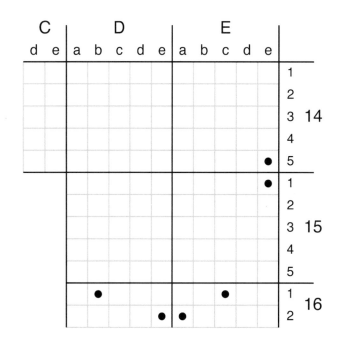

Figure 6.21. The distribution of crude blades (retouched) throughout the lower component (b) of Area C.

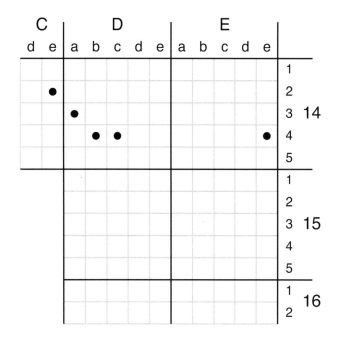

Figure 6.22. The distribution of end scrapers throughout the lower component (b) of Area C.

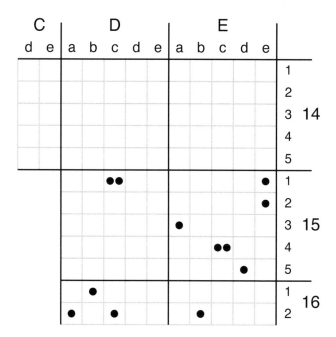

Figure 6.23. The distribution of sidescrapers/knives throughout the lower component (b) of Area C.

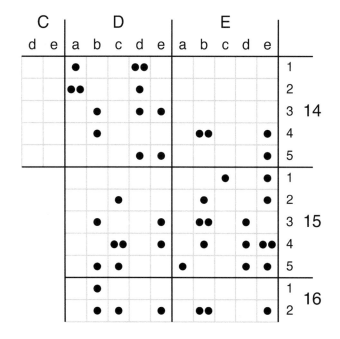

Figure 6.24. The distribution of steep denticulate scrapers throughout the lower component (b) of Area C.

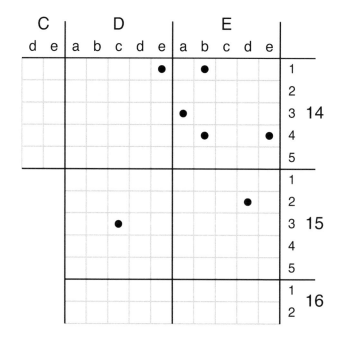

Figure 6.25. The distribution of burins throughout the lower component (b) of Area C.

Chipped Stone Tools: The Horizontal Distribution

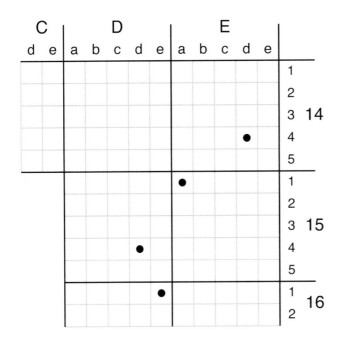

Figure 6.26. The distribution of drills throughout the lower component (b) of Area C.

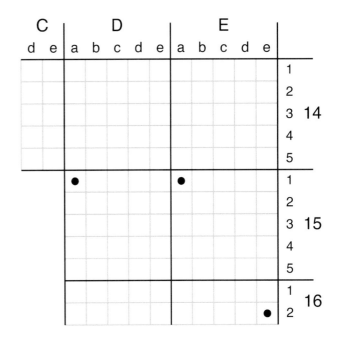

Figure 6.27. The distribution of Variety A bifaces throughout the lower component (b) of Area C.

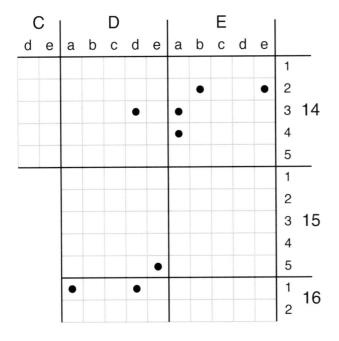

Figure 6.28. The distribution of Variety B bifaces throughout the lower component (b) of Area C.

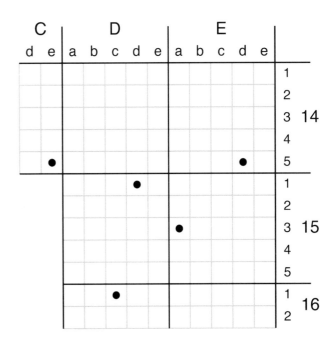

Figure 6.29. The distribution of Variety C bifaces throughout the lower component (b) of Area C.

Summary

While some chipped stone tools from component b display clustering, many do not. For whatever reason, we seem not to have the kinds of strong associations among tool types that could indicate the presence of a hut, a windbreak, or some other area of concentrated activity.

Area C: The Upper Component (a)

We recovered 159 chipped stone tools and 3223 pieces of debitage from the upper component (a) of Area C (Table 6.3); we chose to analyze the distribution of ten chipped stone categories. In our examination of component a, we had two goals in mind. One was to see whether any of the chipped stone tools showed clustering. The other was to compare the tool distributions in component a to those in component b. Among other things, we wanted to see if the tool distributions in b and a were sufficiently different to validate our making them two separate components.

Hammerstones (Figure 6.30). We recovered 12 hammerstones from component a. Four of these formed a semicircle in the southeast corner of Area C. Six more hammerstones were found in the northwest quadrant (Squares C14 and D14), but were not tightly clustered. This distribution does not closely resemble the hammerstone distribution from component b.

Flake cores (Figure 6.31). There were 20 flake cores in component a, distributed very differently from those in component b. We see at least four small clusters (two in Square E15, one in D14, and one at the border of D14 and D15). Each cluster is small enough to represent the activity of one individual.

Debitage (Figure 6.32). We recovered some 3223 pieces of debitage from component a. This debitage was widespread, and we were unable to detect any potential activity areas; nor did the 1 x 1 m squares with the highest debitage counts seem to correspond to those from component b.

Utilized flakes (Figure 6.33). Component a yielded 15 utilized flakes. Four of these were found within a meter of square E14/c5; five were found in the southern half of Square E15. Neither of these potential clusters closely matched the distribution of utilized flakes in component b.

Notched flakes (Figure 6.34). We found 28 notched flakes in component a. Potential clusters included (1) a semicircle of five in the southern half of Square D15 and adjacent D16, and (2) eight in the southern half of Square E15 and adjacent E16. In contrast to their distribution in component b, there were relatively few notched flakes in the northwest quadrant of component a.

Flakes with bulbar end retouch were not recovered from component a; they seem to have been unique to component b.

Crude blades, plain (Figure 6.35). Only five plain blades were found in component a, and no clustering was evident.

Sidescrapers/knives (Figure 6.36). We found only four sidescrapers/knives in component a. We saw no convincing clusters, and the distribution of this tool type was strikingly different from that in component b.

Steep denticulate scrapers (Figure 6.37). We recovered some 20 steep denticulate scrapers from component a. Five of these were found in the extreme northwest corner of Area C. Another seven were found in the southeast quadrant, but did not appear to be tightly clustered. This distribution does not resemble that of component b.

Table 6.3. Chipped stone tools from the upper component (a) of Area C.

Hammerstones	12
Flake cores	20
Core fragments	37
Utilized flakes	15
Notched flakes	28
Flakes with bulbar end retouch	—
Crude blades, plain	5
Crude blades, retouched	—
Flakes with sheen	1
Sickles	—
Choppers	—
End scrapers	—
Sidescrapers/knives	4
Steep denticulate scrapers	20
Burins	9
Drills	2
Bifaces, Variety A	—
Bifaces, Variety B	2
Bifaces, Variety C	1
Projectile points	3
Total	**159**

Chipped Stone Tools: The Horizontal Distribution

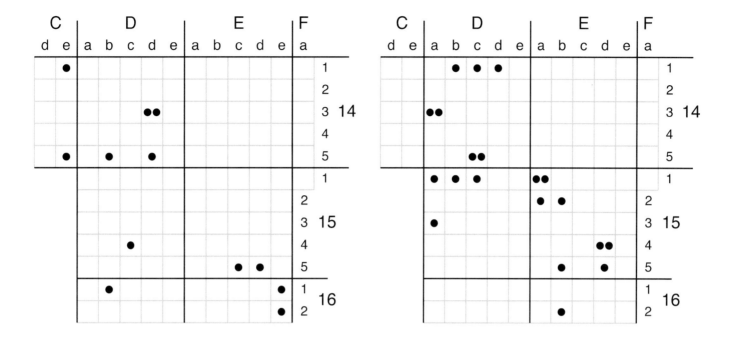

Figure 6.30. The distribution of hammerstones throughout the upper component (a) of Area C.

Figure 6.31. The distribution of flake cores throughout the upper component (a) of Area C.

Figure 6.32. The distribution of debitage throughout the upper component (a) of Area C, by 1 x 1 m square.

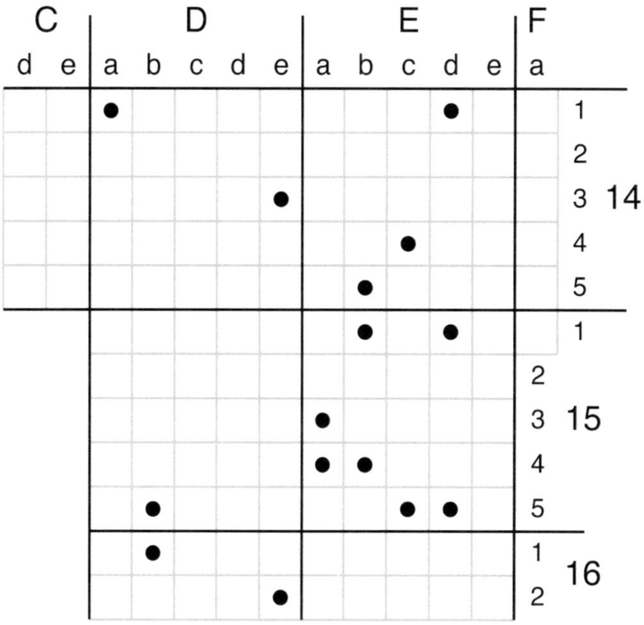

Figure 6.33. The distribution of utilized flakes throughout the upper component (a) of Area C.

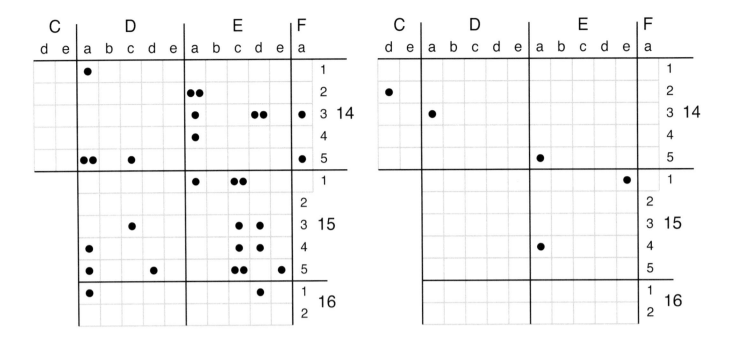

Figure 6.34. The distribution of notched flakes throughout the upper component (a) of Area C.

Figure 6.35. The distribution of crude blades (plain) throughout the upper component (a) of Area C.

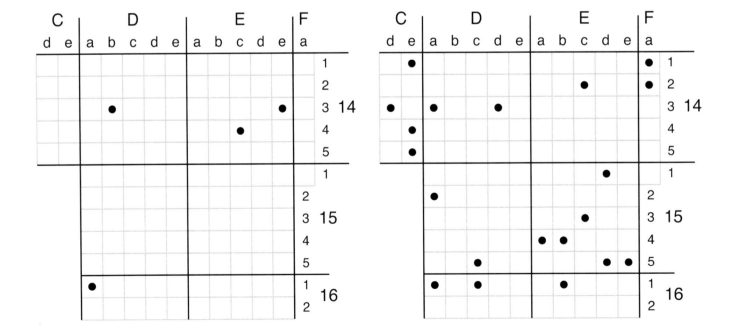

Figure 6.36. The distribution of sidescrapers/knives throughout the upper component (a) of Area C.

Figure 6.37. The distribution of steep denticulate scrapers throughout the upper component (a) of Area C.

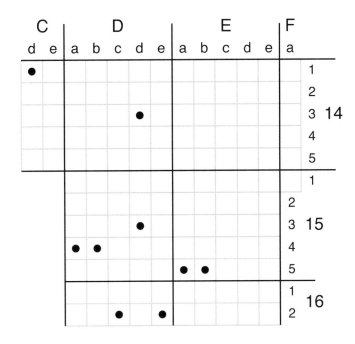

Figure 6.38. The distribution of burins throughout the upper component (a) of Area C.

Burins (Figure 6.38). We recovered nine burins from component a. Seven of these were found in the southern part of Area C, in what could possibly represent a large work area. There was virtually no overlap between this distribution and that of the burins found in component b.

Summary

Component a produced a smaller sample of chipped stone tools than component b; many types, in fact, were so rare that their distributions were not worth plotting. A few tools demonstrated possible clustering, but most did not.

We find it significant that the tool distributions from components a and b were very different. Recall that there was no strongly visible soil change at a depth of 20 cm, where we established the break between component a (0–20 cm) and component b (usually 20–40 cm, except in places where there were natural depressions). In cases where there is no natural stratigraphic break, one always worries that he or she has arbitrarily divided a single occupation into two. In this case, the clear differences in tool distributions between components a and b suggest that we are, in fact, dealing with two different occupations. In addition, each component had a few unique features—stone-lined hearths in the case of component a, and a cluster of flakes with bulbar retouch in the case of component b.

Conclusions

Area C was characterized by two superimposed occupation layers, with projectile point types dating both to the Jícaras phase (see Chapter 7). While these two occupations produced a few artifact clusters that could represent work areas, we found no clear evidence of residential structures or ritual areas in Area C. As we suggested in our discussion of Area A, one of the reasons activity areas were hard to identify may be that both components of Area C were palimpsests of multiple activities, carried out over periods of time longer than that of a typical cave occupation.

Chapter 7

Projectile Points: The Typology

Gheo-Shih provided us with 50 projectile points or fragments thereof, the largest collection from any Archaic site in the Mitla region. Roughly three-quarters of those points were recovered from the surface. Thirty-three of these came from the 5 x 5 m squares of Hole's systematic surface pickup grid; two more were found at times when the stakes defining the grid were not in place. Three additional points were recovered from the dirt road immediately to the north of the grid, bringing the total number of points found on the surface to 38.

Twelve projectile points were found in situ during the excavation of Areas A and C. A total of three came from Area A. Three more came from the upper component (a) of Area C; finally, six points came from the lower component (b) of the same area. That brought the total number of points from Gheo-Shih to 50.

Most, but not all, of the Gheo-Shih points were made of chert or chalcedony. This finer raw material came from farther away than the silicified tuff used for choppers and scrapers.

Not all the points from Gheo-Shih could be classified. Some were only fragments and lacked critical diagnostic features. Others had clearly been "rejuvenated" after suffering damage; as discussed in our volume on Cueva Blanca (Flannery and Hole 2019:102–103), extensive reworking of a damaged point can render it unclassifiable, or even cause it to resemble another point type. As a result, only 30 of the 50 projectile points from Gheo-Shih were classifiable. Of these, 23 were of the Pedernales type. The remaining seven consisted of two San Nicolás points, two Trinidad points, one Hidalgo point, one Abasolo point, and one Palmillas point.

The fact that three-quarters of the classifiable points from Gheo-Shih could be assigned to the Pedernales type caught us by surprise. In no other Archaic assemblage from the Mitla region was one point type so dominant. Given the sites excavated so far, we conclude that the Pedernales point is a useful diagnostic marker of the Jícaras phase. Based on comparisons with Guilá Naquitz and Cueva Blanca, we can suggest that Pedernales points made their first appearance at the very end of the Naquitz phase (cal. 6000 BC). They clearly peaked in popularity during the Jícaras phase (cal. 6000–4000 BC). By the time of the Blanca phase, however (cal. 4000–2300 BC), their popularity had waned; for example, not a single Pedernales point was found in Zones D and C of Cueva Blanca (Flannery and Hole 2019:200).

Although limited in number, the remaining point types essentially support the lessons learned from Guilá Naquitz and Cueva Blanca. Our lone Palmillas point comes from the lower component (b) of Area C. This type, already used during the Naquitz phase, continued to be made until Late Archaic times. Our San Nicolás and Trinidad points were all recovered from the surface; none were found in the lower component (b) of Area C. Our guess is that these two types first appeared late in the Middle Archaic Jícaras phase and increased in frequency during the Late Archaic Blanca phase (Flannery and Hole 2019). During the Late Archaic they were accompanied by La Mina and Tilapa points, neither of which were recovered from Gheo-Shih.[1] All our projectile point evidence, in other words, suggests that even though the initial use of Gheo-Shih may have occurred late in the Naquitz phase, the bulk of the occupation dates to the Jícaras phase.

Point Types

Pedernales points (Figures 7.1–7.14)

Pedernales points have a broad blade with slightly convex edges, and their shoulders are usually marked by fairly prominent barbs. Their most distinctive feature, however, is the stem, which is short and straight with a distinctive concave base. Pedernales points from the Mitla region, while largely percussion flaked, may have careful secondary retouch along the blade edges and the basal concavity of the stem. Sometimes this retouch appears on the alternate sides of opposing edges, a feature also seen on projectile points from the Tehuacán Valley.[2]

Figure 7.1 presents the reader with a complete, largely undamaged Pedernales point. This particular point was found on the surface near Guilá Naquitz Cave, and illustrates what such points looked like before they had been damaged and reworked. This point likely dates to the Jícaras phase; five maize cobs from that phase were recovered from Guilá Naquitz (see Chapter 11).

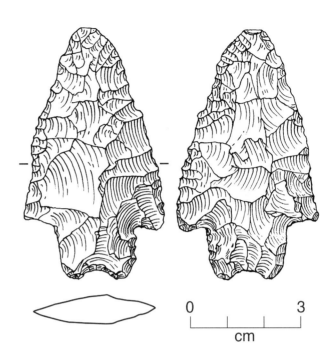

Figure 7.1. This Pedernales point, found on the surface near Guilá Naquitz Cave, is our most complete and undamaged example of the type.

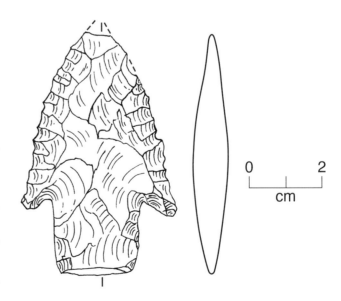

Figure 7.2. Slightly damaged Pedernales point from the lower component (b) of Area C. This point was found in square E15/e1.

---

1. In an earlier publication (Flannery and Marcus 2015:7), Flannery raised the possibility that a La Mina point might have been present at Gheo-Shih. After further examination, we have relegated that point fragment to the "unclassified" category.
2. The Pedernales point was originally identified in Texas, where (according to our Texas colleagues) it is usually pronounced "Perd-nallis."

Figure 7.3. Pedernales point from the surface of Gheo-Shih; its blade had been damaged and skillfully rejuvenated.

Figure 7.4. Damaged Pedernales point recovered from the surface of Gheo-Shih by J. Marcus in 1972, five years after Hole's excavation. At this point, the site had returned to being an agave field.

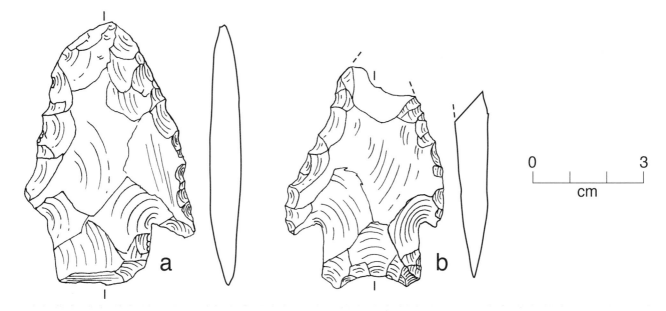

Figure 7.5. Two damaged Pedernales points from the surface of Gheo-Shih. *a* was found in Square CC29; *b* was found in Square DD31.

None of the Pedernales points from Gheo-Shih were as complete as the one shown in Figure 7.1. Our most nearly complete example is a point found in the lower component (b) of Area C (Figure 7.2); it is missing only the tip of the blade and the concave base of the stem. Figure 7.3 shows a point from the surface of Gheo-Shih whose blade had been skillfully rejuvenated; its stem and barbs are intact.

Figures 7.4 through 7.6 illustrate damaged Pedernales points; Figures 7.7 and 7.8 show heavily reworked specimens. Additional damaged and/or reworked specimens can be seen in Figures 7.9 through 7.13. Finally, Figure 7.14 presents five diagnostic stems from broken Pedernales points.

Trinidad points (Figures 7.15, 7.16)

Trinidad points are broad-bladed and have relatively short, wide contracting stems with convex bases. Their bodies, which are longer than the stems, are roughly the shape of an isosceles triangle and have slightly convex edges. The

Projectile Points: The Typology

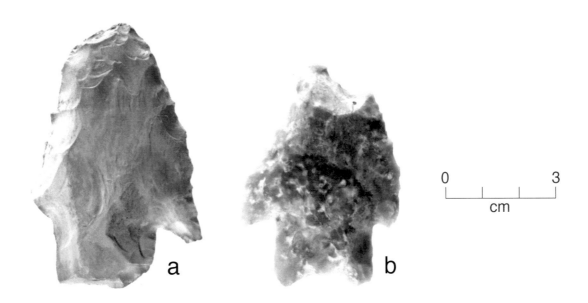

Figure 7.6. Photographs of the same two Pedernales points shown in Figure 7.5.

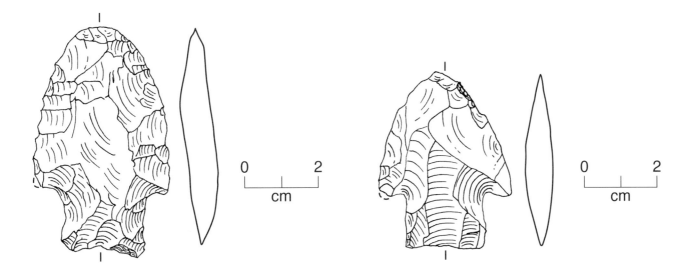

Figure 7.7. Reworked Pedernales point, found on the dirt road just north of Gheo-Shih.

Figure 7.8. Extensively reworked Pedernales point from the surface of Gheo-Shih (Square L23).

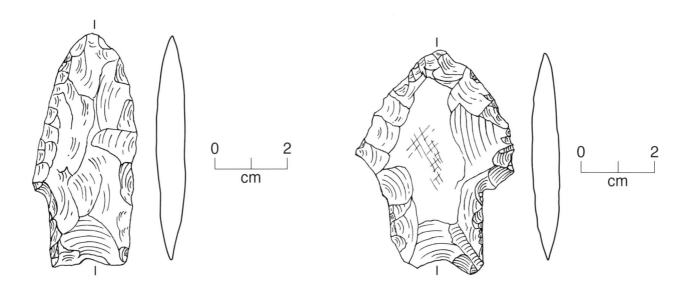

Figure 7.9. Damaged Pedernales point from the Jícaras phase component of Area A.

Figure 7.10. Heavily reworked Pedernales point from the Jícaras phase component of Area A.

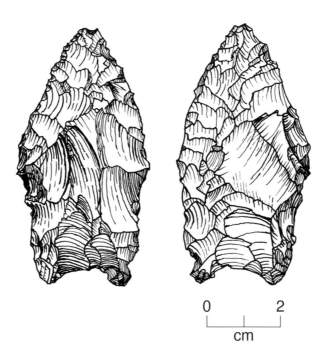

Figure 7.11. Damaged Pedernales point from the surface of Gheo-Shih (Square H26).

Projectile Points: The Typology

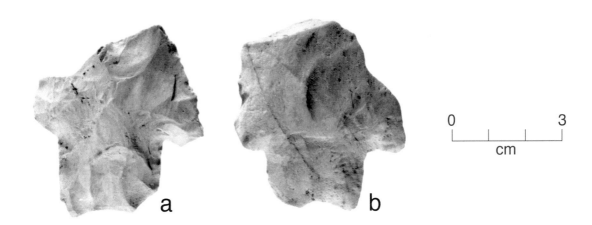

Figure 7.12. Two damaged Pedernales points from the surface of Gheo-Shih. *a* was found in Square AA26; *b* was found in Square K1.

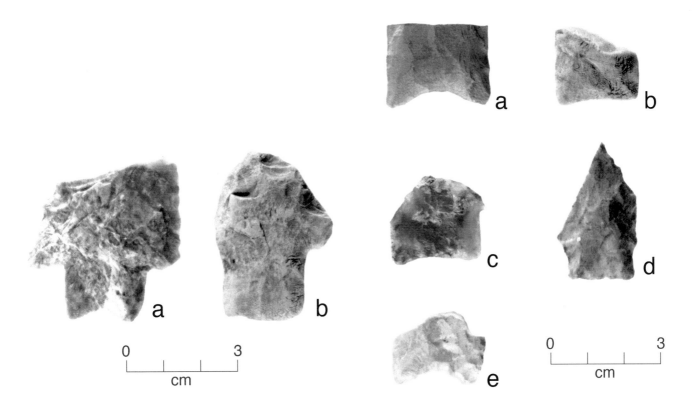

Figure 7.13. Two damaged Pedernales points from the surface of Gheo-Shih. *a* was found in Square AA24; *b* was found in Square Q14.

Figure 7.14. Stems from broken Pedernales points, recovered from the surface of Gheo-Shih. *a*, Square DD28. *b*, Square Q14. *c*, Square G2. *d*, Square B20. *e*, Square N1.

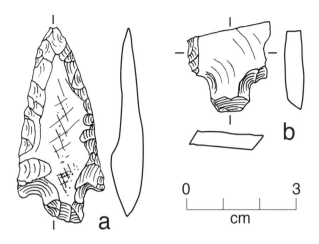

Figure 7.15. Two Trinidad points from the surface of Gheo-Shih. *a* is a slightly damaged point from Square H28, which later became part of Area A. *b* is the proximal half of a badly damaged point from Square K22.

Figure 7.16. Photographs of the same two Trinidad points shown in Figure 7.15.

shoulders are usually marked with fairly prominent short barbs (MacNeish et al. 1967:62).

We recovered two damaged Trinidad points from the surface of Gheo-Shih (Figures 7.15 and 7.16). Given the likelihood that most of the material on the surface had eroded out of the upper components of the site, these Trinidad points likely date to the Jícaras phase. Contracting-stem points were present throughout the Archaic sequence in the Mitla region, but the Trinidad type seems to have reached its peak popularity during the Blanca phase (Flannery and Hole 2019).

San Nicolás points (Figures 7.17, 7.18)

These are long, narrow points with short, wide contracting stems and convex to almost pointed bases. As MacNeish et al. (1967:63) put it, "The shoulder where the stem joins the body is not well marked; at most, there is a short step roughly at right angles to the main axis."

Only two San Nicolás points were found at Gheo-shih, and both were recovered from the surface (Figures 7.17 and 7.18). Compared to the San Nicolás points from Cueva Blanca (Flannery and Hole 2019: Fig. 6.7), the two from Gheo-Shih look slightly atypical. In both cases, however, this impression may be the result of damage and repair; each of the points appears to have had one shoulder damaged, and the one found in Square E15 also appears to have suffered damage to its stem.

Our evidence suggests that in the Mitla region, San Nicolás points made their first appearance in the Jícaras phase and reached peak popularity in the Blanca phase.

Palmillas point (Figure 7.19)

Palmillas points are corner-notched, giving them an expanding stem with a convex base. The blade is usually shaped like an equilateral triangle, although reworking after damage can alter the shape.

Palmillas points were used throughout the Archaic sequence in the Mitla region, but seem never to have become particularly numerous. A single point of this type was recovered from the lower component (b) of Area C at Gheo-Shih (Figure 7.19).

Hidalgo point (Figures 7.20, 7.21)

Hidalgo points are one of the most problematic of MacNeish et al.'s (1967:61) Tehuacán Valley types. These points have contracting stems that are as long as—or longer than—their blades. As we discussed in the Cueva Blanca report (Flannery and Hole 2019:105), our suspicion is that these unusual proportions are the result of extensive point

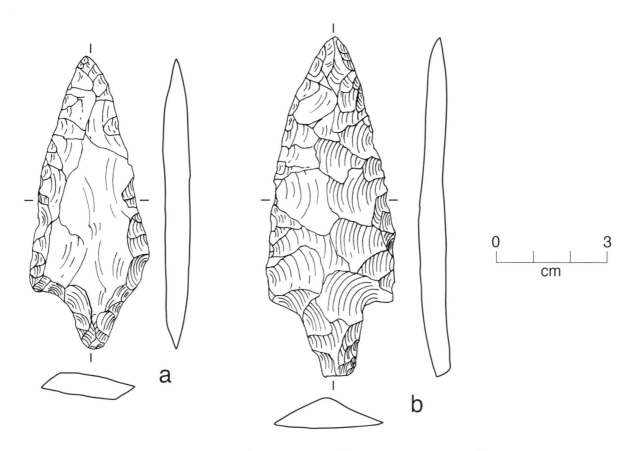

Figure 7.17. Two San Nicolás points from the surface of Gheo-Shih. *a* was found in Square B14; *b* was found in Square E15, which later became part of Area C.

Figure 7.18. Photographs of the same two San Nicolás points shown in Figure 7.17. *b* appears to be made of chalcedony.

Figure 7.19. Badly broken Palmillas point from the lower component (b) of Area C.

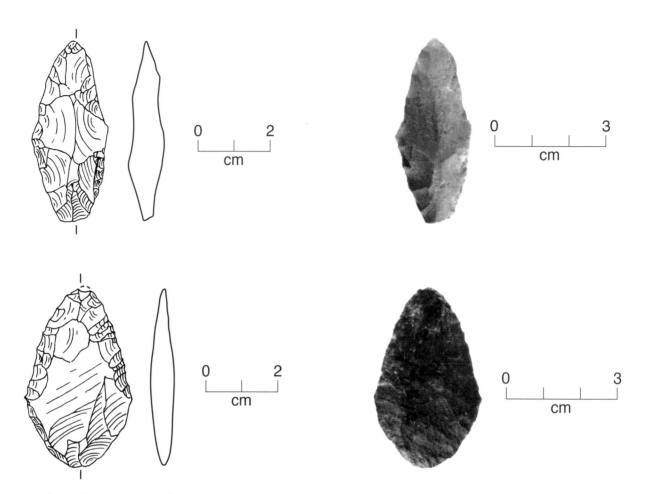

Figure 7.20 (top left). Hidalgo point from the lower component (b) of Area C. Figure 7.21 (top right). Photograph of the same Hidalgo point shown in Figure 7.20. Figure 7.22 (above left). Abasolo point from the upper component (a) of Area C; it appears to have been created by reworking the blade of a broken Pedernales point. Figure 7.23 (above right). Photograph of the same Abasolo point shown in Figure 7.22.

rejuvenation. In fact, we suspect that most, if not all, Hidalgo points were once contracting-stem points of other types, whose blades were extensively reworked following damage.

Only one Hidalgo point was recovered from Gheo-Shih; it was found in the lower component (b) of Area C (Figures 7.20 and 7.21). This point, like so many of its type, appears to have been extensively reworked.

Abasolo point (Figures 7.22, 7.23)

Abasolo points are almond-shaped and have no stem. In the words of MacNeish et al. (1967:57), they have "the outline of a tear drop, with rounded bases, slightly convex sides, and tapering tips." This point type was relatively rare in the Archaic of the Mitla region, and often appears to have been reworked from the blade of another point after damage (Flannery and Hole 2019: Fig. 6.10 b).

Only one Abasolo point was recovered from Gheo-Shih; it came from the upper component (a) of Area C (Figures 7.22 and 7.23). While it satisfies the morphological criteria for an Abasolo point, it appears to have been made by rejuvenating the blade of a broken Pedernales point. Figure 7.22 shows that the upper half of the point displays the fine secondary retouch of a Pedernales point, while its lower half appears improvised.

The Popularity of Pedernales Points

The popularity of Pedernales points can be seen in the projectile point collections from Area A, the lower component of Area C, and the upper component of Area C (Figures 7.24–7.26). Of the 12 projectile points recovered

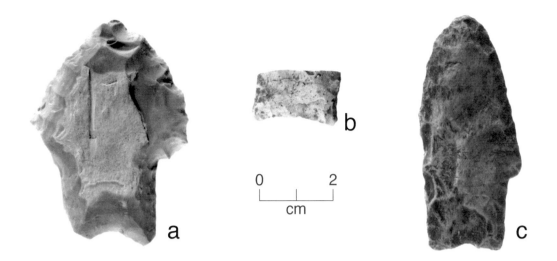

Figure 7.24. Projectile points from the Jícaras phase component of Area A; all are Pedernales points or fragments thereof. *a*, heavily reworked point from square H25/a5. *b*, broken stem from square F29/c4. *c*, damaged point from square G29/c2.

Figure 7.25. Projectile points from the lower component (b) of Area C. *a*, Pedernales point from square E15/e1. *b*, likely stem of a Pedernales point from square D15/b2. *c*, badly damaged Pedernales point from square D14/e3. *d*, damaged Palmillas point from square D14/c2. *e*, Hidalgo point from square E14/a2. *f*, unclassified point fragment from square E15/c3.

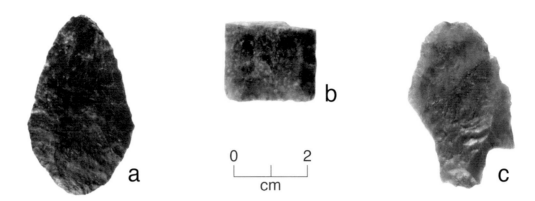

Figure 7.26. Projectile points from the upper component (a) of Area C. *a*, Abasolo point from square C14/e2. *b*, stem from a broken Pedernales point, square D15/c5. *c*, unclassified barbed and stemmed point from square C14/e4.

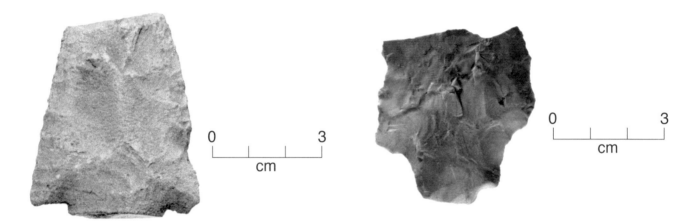

Figure 7.27. Unclassified, badly broken point from the surface of Gheo-Shih (Square B18).

Figure 7.28. The proximal half of an unclassified, badly broken point from the surface (Square S6).

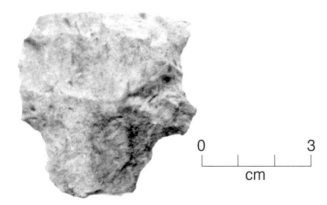

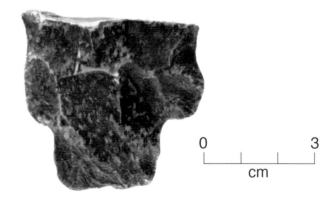

Figure 7.29. Unclassified, badly broken point from the surface (Square F5).

Figure 7.30. The proximal half of an unclassified, badly weathered point from the surface (Square B32).

from those contexts, at least seven were likely Pedernales points (or fragments thereof).

Unclassified Points

In addition to the 30 classified points from Gheo-Shih, there were 20 points (or fragments thereof) that could not be assigned to types. These were, for the most part, points damaged in such a way that they lacked critical diagnostic features. We illustrate many of these points in Figures 7.27 through 7.34.

At least five of our unclassified points might, if only they were undamaged, be classifiable as the Pedernales type (Figures 7.27–7.31). Another of the unclassified points might once have belonged to the Trinidad type, but lacks the diagnostic stem and barbs (Figure 7.33). Significantly, our unclassified points provide little evidence for types other than Pedernales, Trinidad, San Nicolás, Palmillas, Hidalgo, or Abasolo.

Discussion

Gheo-Shih provides us with our best look at the Middle Archaic Jícaras phase. It appears that the most popular point type of that phase was the Pedernales point. This type made its first appearance toward the end of the Naquitz phase, peaked in Jícaras, and seems not to have lasted into the Late Archaic Blanca phase.

Of the other point types from Gheo-Shih, one (Palmillas corner-notched) was used throughout the Archaic of the Mitla region. Two other point types, Trinidad and San Nicolás, reached their peak popularity during the Late Archaic Blanca phase. The two remaining point types from Gheo-Shih—Hidalgo and Abasolo—are less useful for establishing chronologies, because they so often appear to have resulted from the post-damage reworking of another point type.

Finally, we find it significant that two Late Archaic point types, Tilapa and Coxcatlán, were not recovered from Gheo-Shih.

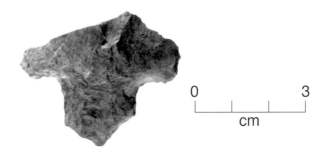

Figure 7.31. Unclassified, badly broken point from the surface (Square J1).

Figure 7.32. Unclassified projectile point fragments from the surface of Gheo-Shih. *a*, blade fragment from Square H8. *b*, blade fragment from Square H3. *c*, blade fragment from Square O21. *d*, barb and damaged stem from Square C11.

Figure 7.33. Distal end of a projectile point from the surface (Square R9).

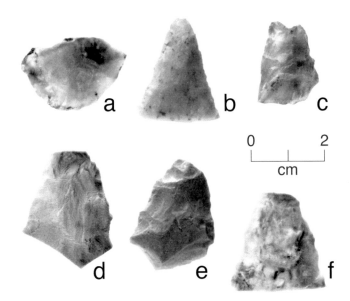

Figure 7.34. Projectile point fragments from the surface of Gheo-Shih. *a*, possible base of an Abasolo point from Square L7. *b*, point tip from Square BB32. *c*, point tip from Square EE28. *d*, blade fragment from Square C9. *e*, blade fragment from Square D12. *f*, point tip from Square Q11.

Chapter 8

Projectile Points: The Horizontal Distribution

Only 12 of our 50 projectile points from Gheo-Shih were found in situ during the excavation of Areas A and C. The fact that these points had stratigraphic context and could be fixed three-dimensionally in space, however, gives them special significance.

Area A

No points were recovered from the basal level of Area A. The presence of Feature 1 in this area suggests that during the late Naquitz phase, this part of Gheo-Shih was devoted more to ritual activity than to subsistence or crafts.

Three projectile points or fragments thereof were recovered from the upper component of Area A (Figure 8.1). All could be assigned to the Pedernales type, confirming the fact that the upper component fell squarely in the Jícaras phase. The Pedernales points from Area A can be seen in Figures 7.9, 7.10, and 7.24 of Chapter 7. All three points were damaged or extensively reworked, suggesting that this was an area where used (perhaps even heavily used) points were discarded, rather than an area where new points were being made.

Area C: The Lower Component

The lower component (b) of Area C yielded six projectile points or fragments thereof (Figure 8.2). While these points were not sufficiently clustered to suggest the presence of an activity area, neither were they widely scattered. Two came from Square D14, two from Square E15, and the remaining two from Squares D15 and E14. Three of the points could be assigned to the Pedernales type; the other three consisted of one Palmillas point, one Hidalgo point, and one unclassified fragment.

All of these points can be seen in Figures 7.2, 7.19, 7.20, 7.21, and 7.25 of Chapter 7. One of the Pedernales points

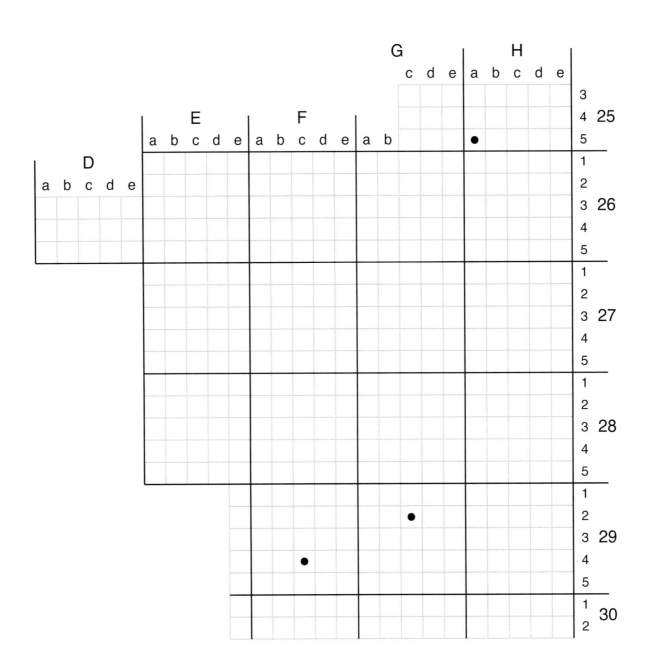

Figure 8.1. The distribution of projectile points throughout the Jícaras phase component of Area A.

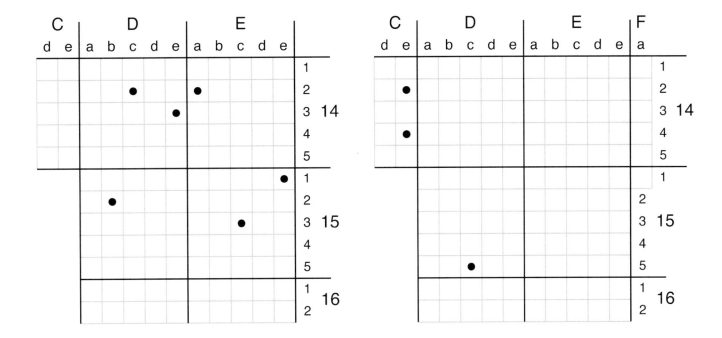

Figure 8.2. The distribution of projectile points throughout the lower component (b) of Area C.

Figure 8.3. The distribution of projectile points throughout the upper component (a) of Area C.

appears to be only lightly damaged; as for the Hidalgo point, see our discussion of this type in Chapter 7. The remaining four specimens are fragments or badly damaged points.

Area C: The Upper Component

The upper component (a) of Area C produced three points or fragments thereof (Figure 8.3). All were found in the western part of Area C, but did not form a cluster. Their distribution did not in any way resemble that of the projectile points in component b. One point could be assigned to the Pedernales type, the second was an Abasolo point, and the third was too damaged to classify. These three points can be seen in Figures 7.23 and 7.26 of Chapter 7.

Chapter 9

Ground Stone Tools

We recovered only a few complete ground stone tools from Gheo-Shih. There were, however, dozens of fragments of metates or manos that had broken during use.

Manos

All the manos or mano fragments we recovered were of the simple one-hand type, usually made from ignimbrite stream cobbles of the appropriate size. This type was described in the Guilá Naquitz Cave report (Flannery 2009a:147–148) as follows:

> For the most part, these were rough-and-ready tools made from ignimbrite cobbles picked up in a stream bed and shaped as much by stream action and use as by design. Any of them could have been picked up at the beginning of a cave occupation, used conveniently in one hand by either a man or woman, and discarded at the end of the occupation with the knowledge that a replacement would be easy to find.

Metates

In all cases, the Gheo-Shih metates were simple slabs of coarse stone, without prominent rims or worn basins. They therefore fit the definition of the slab metates found at Guilá Naquitz (Flannery 2009:151), which are described as follows:

> These roughly shaped thin slabs of volcanic tuff have a single flat or slightly concave grinding surface. The bottom of the slab is pecked to form an uneven but generally flat surface. None … show any evidence of deliberately finished edges.

Pestles

Only one possible pestle fragment was recovered, and that happened during the excavation of Jícaras phase deposits in Area A. We recovered no fragments of mortars, suggesting that their use was rare.

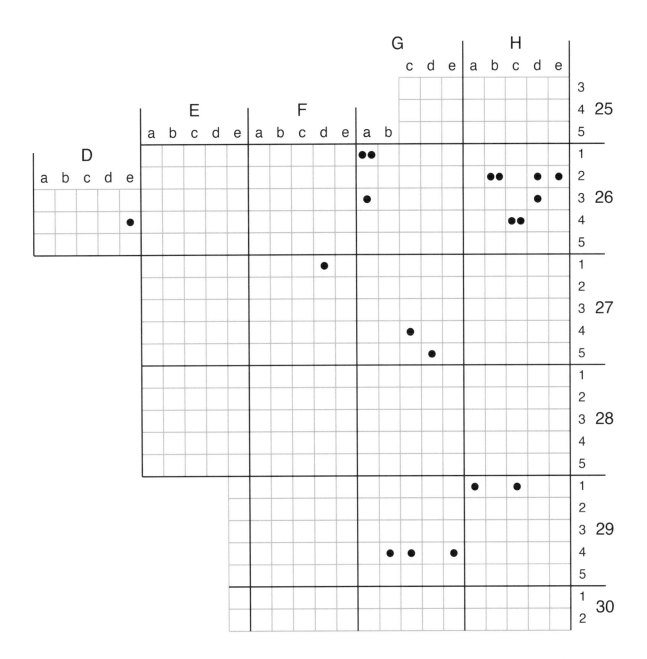

Figure 9.1. The distribution of manos and mano fragments throughout the Jícaras phase component of Area A.

Possible Stone Bowl

One possible fragment of a crude stone bowl was recovered during the excavation of Area A. Stone bowls were rare in the Archaic of the Mitla region; with the exception of this possible fragment from the Jícaras phase, they are known only from Terminal Archaic levels at the Martínez Rockshelter (Flannery and Spores 2003:25). No stone bowls (or fragments thereof) were recovered from Blanca-phase levels at Cueva Blanca (Flannery and Hole 2019).

Horizontal Distribution of the Ground Stone Tools

Area A: The Jícaras Phase Deposits

Some 19 one-hand manos or fragments thereof were recovered from the Jícaras phase component of Area A (Figure 9.1). Roughly half of these were found in the northeast quadrant of Area A; the most striking cluster

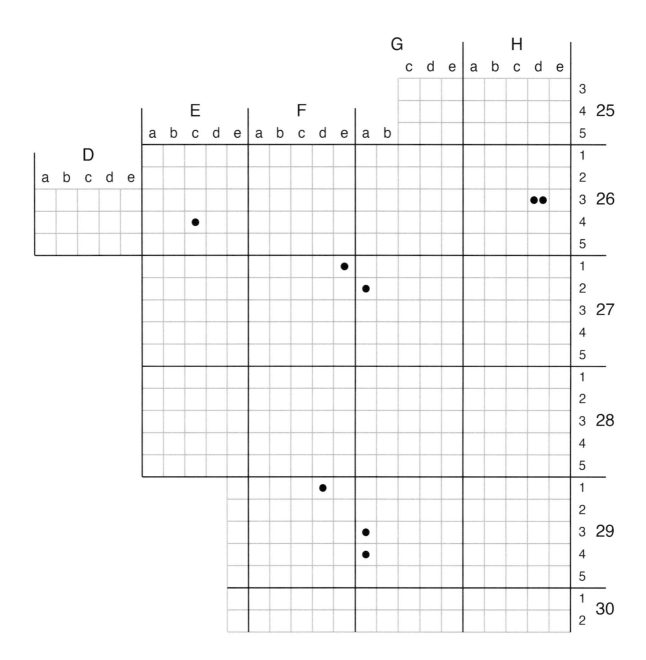

Figure 9.2. The distribution of metate fragments throughout the Jícaras phase component of Area A.

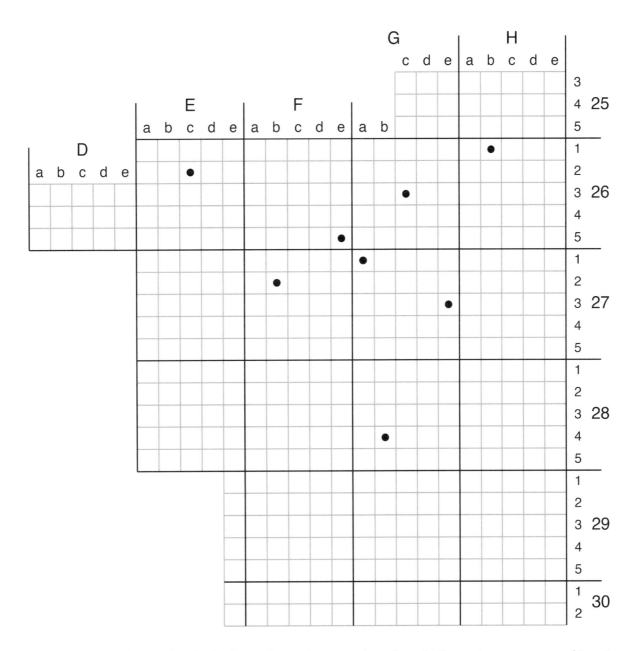

Figure 9.3. The distribution of unclassified ground stone fragments throughout the Jícaras phase component of Area A.

consists of seven items from 5 x 5 m Square H26. Given that two metate fragments also occurred in H26, it is possible that this was an area where grinding activity took place.

Only eight slab metate fragments were recovered from the Jícaras deposits in Area A (Figure 9.2). There is little evidence for clustering except in the case of the two fragments mentioned above, which were found with a group of manos.

Eight additional fragments of ground stone, too incomplete to classify, were found in the Jícaras phase component of Area A (Figure 9.3). One of these occurred in Square H26, where a potential cluster of metate and mano fragments has already been noted.

Finally, Figure 9.4 shows the location of possible pestle and stone bowl fragments in the Jícaras phase component of Area A.

Area C: The Lower Component (b)

Let us turn now to the distribution of ground stone items in Area C, beginning with the lower stratigraphic component

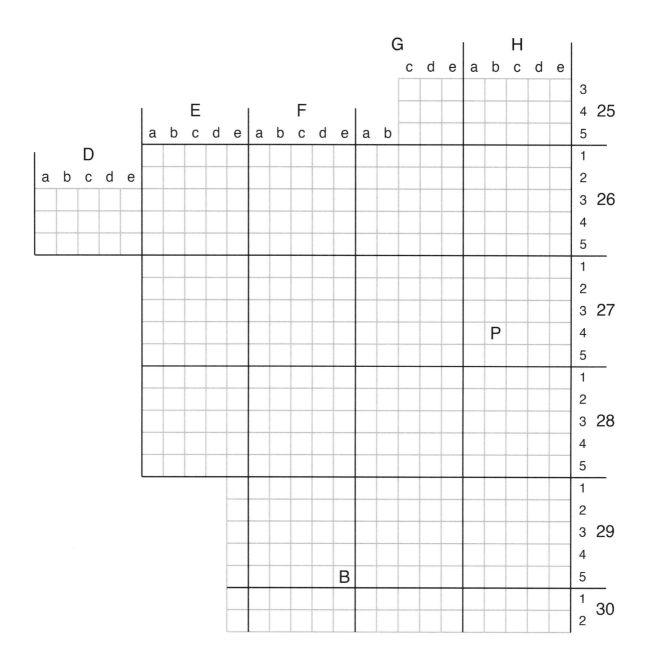

Figure 9.4. The proveniences of a possible pestle (P) and stone bowl fragment (B) in the Jícaras phase component of Area A.

(b). Some 10 one-hand manos or fragments thereof were recovered from component b (Figure 9.5). Six of these occurred in the northeast quadrant, but no obvious clusters are evident. A possible cluster of three can be seen in the south, at the juncture of 5 x 5 m Squares E15 and E16. Reinforcing this possibility is the fact that our only metate fragment from component b was found in square E15/b5, and could thus be considered part of the same cluster. We can therefore suggest that there may have been a grinding activity area in the southern part of component b.

Finally, one ambiguous ground stone fragment that could have come from either a mano or a metate was recovered from square E14/c4.

Area C: The Upper Component (a)

Only eight manos or fragments thereof were recovered from the upper component a of Area C (Figure 9.6). Their distribution does not closely match component b's, suggesting that our stratigraphic separation of components a and b did not result in the arbitrary subdivision of a natural stratigraphic level. It is, however, the case that half of the manos/mano fragments were found in the northeast quadrant of Area A, a locality which (for one reason or another) seems to have had more than its share of tool discard (see Chapter 6).

Finally, no clear fragments of slab metates, pestles, or stone bowls were found in component a of Area C.

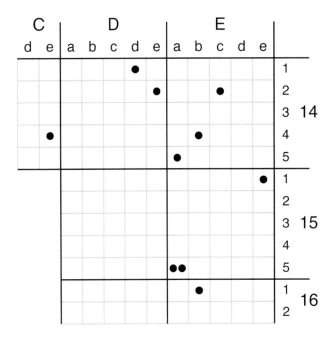

Figure 9.5. The distribution of manos and mano fragments throughout the lower component (b) of Area C.

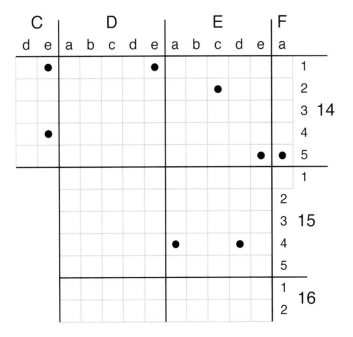

Figure 9.6. The distribution of manos and mano fragments throughout the upper component (a) of Area C.

Chapter 10

Ornaments

Gheo-Shih was unique—at least, among the excavated Archaic sites of the Mitla region— in that it provided us with evidence of local ornament manufacture. To be sure, some of our other Archaic sites yielded isolated ornaments, such as the marine shell from Cueva Blanca (Flannery and Hole 2019: Figure 3.8). Only Gheo-Shih, however, shows us the manufacture of ornaments from local raw material; equally importantly, the working of each ornament type seems to have been restricted to one part of the site.

We are aware that our sample of Archaic sites is small, and that Gheo-Shih is our only excavated example of an open-air macroband camp. Even this limited evidence, however, allows us to propose two hypotheses for future testing: (1) that most Archaic ornament manufacture occurred at times when 25–50 people were living together in a macroband camp, and (2) that only certain families, or groups of residents, engaged in this activity.

Let us now look at Gheo-Shih's two types of locally made ornaments: oval pendants and biconically drilled stone discs.

Oval Pendants

Two examples of oval pendants were recovered, both from Area A. Both had been made on similar pink pebbles, carefully ground until they were thin enough to be worn as pendants. A small hole for suspension was then drilled near one end of each pendant (Figure 10.1).

Our one complete pendant was roughly 4 cm long and 2.7 cm wide; its hole for suspension was just under 3 mm wide, although the cavity left by biconical drilling was larger at its rim. The second pendant was too broken to measure, but we can say that its hole for suspension was less than 2 mm in diameter.

Figure 10.2 shows the location of both pendants in Area A.

Biconically Drilled Stone Discs

Five examples of biconically drilled stone discs were recovered from Jícaras phase deposits in Area C; one piece from a sixth disc was found on the surface of the site during the systematic pickup.

All of our biconically drilled discs were made from the same tan, sandy, laminated stone. While it cannot be confirmed without trace element analysis, we strongly suspect that the source of this stone was an area of sandstones and marls some four to six kilometers southwest of Gheo-Shih, in the foothills on the opposite side of the Río Mitla (Whalen 2009: Figure 7.1). This area was also a potential source of silicified sedimentary rock for chipped stone tools.

It appears that the ornament makers selected already-thin pebbles of this raw material, then ground them on both faces to thin them further. They next ground the edges until the pebbles were roughly circular. Finally, a hole for suspension was biconically drilled near the center of the disc. There were signs that discs occasionally broke during the process of drilling, which may have been carried out with chert drills like those shown in Chapter 5 (see Figure 5.63). We note that four of these drills were found in the lower component (b) of Area C (see Figure 6.26), which is where the bulk of our biconically drilled discs were found.

Our complete specimens of biconically drilled discs range in diameter from 2.85 cm to 4.67 cm; their thickness varies from 0.35 cm to 0.50 cm. The diameter of the hole drilled for suspension ranges from 0.27 cm to 0.40 cm, although the cavity left by biconical drilling is larger at its rim (see Figures 10.3–10.5).

We believe that these centrally drilled discs were ornaments, although we are not sure whether they were worn singly (as pendants) or strung together in groups (as necklaces). We briefly considered—and rejected—the possibility that they were spindle whorls, for the following reasons: (1) they are far too heavy for this purpose, and the central hole is too small to accommodate a spindle; and (2) most documented Mesoamerican spindle whorls are small, spherical, and made of wood or ceramics.

Four of our biconically drilled stone discs (Figures 10.4, 10.5) were recovered from the lower component (b) of Area C; their locations are given in Figure 10.6. As mentioned above, four of the chert drills that may have been used to drill the central holes in these ornaments were found in the same component. Since Area A produced none of these discs, it would appear that only the residents of Area C were involved in their manufacture.

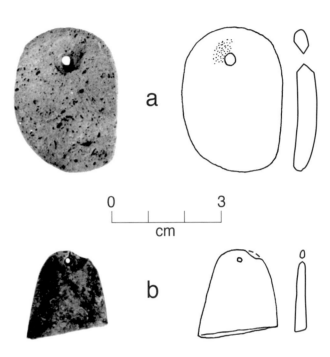

Figure 10.1. Two oval stone pendants recovered from the Jícaras phase component of Area A. *a*, photo and drawing of a complete pendant from square E26/a4. *b*, photo and drawing of a broken pendant from square E28/b1.

124 Chapter 10

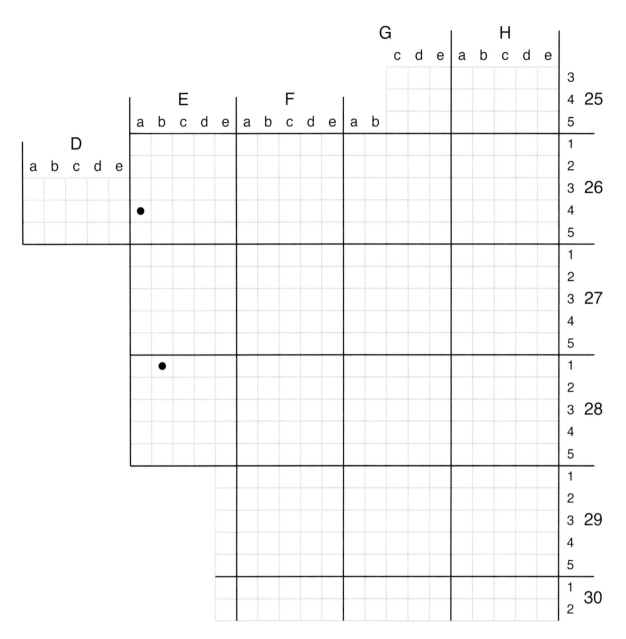

Figure 10.2. The distribution of oval pendants throughout the Jícaras phase component of Area A.

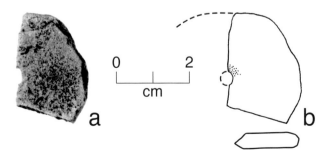

Figure 10.3. A fragment of biconically drilled disc recovered from the surface of Gheo-Shih (Square C9).

Ornaments

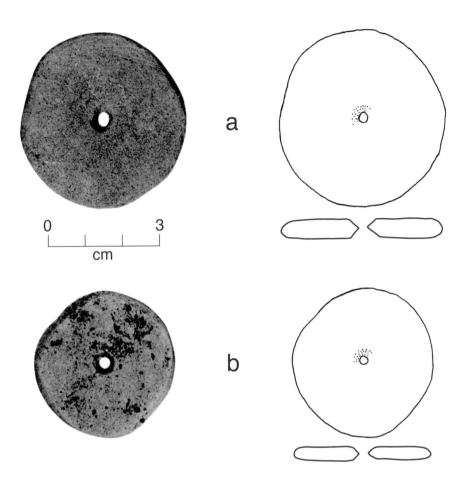

Figure 10.4. Two biconically drilled stone discs recovered from the lower component (b) of Area C. *a*, photo and drawing of disc from square E14/d4. *b*, photo and drawing of disc from square D15/b5.

One additional biconically drilled stone disc was found in the upper component (a) of Area C (Figure 10.7). We are uncertain whether this means that ornament manufacture continued during the occupation of component a, or whether this stone disc was simply redeposited in component a as the result of pit digging or some other disturbance; we suspect the latter. This disc from component a was found in square E15/e3 (Figure 10.8).

Discussion

Two types of ornaments, likely made on local raw material, were found in Jícaras phase deposits at Gheo-Shih. Four biconically drilled discs of tan, sandy, laminated stone were found in component b of Area C, along with four chert drills that could have been used to make the central hole. Two oval pendants, made from pink pebbles, were recovered from Area A. Since we discovered no comparable evidence of ornament manufacture at any of the small family microband camps of the Mitla Archaic, it would seem that ornament making was most often carried out at macroband camps.

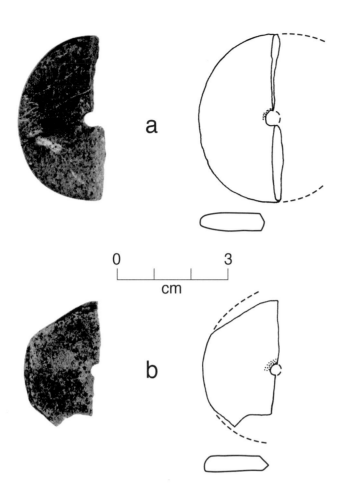

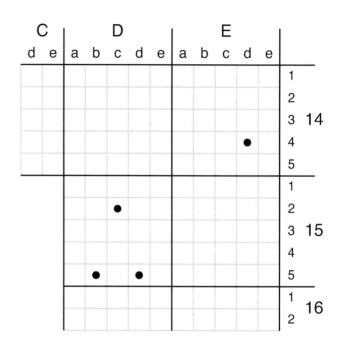

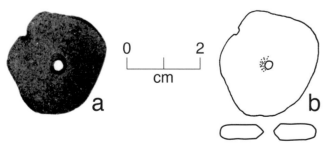

Figure 10.5. Two biconically drilled stone discs from the lower component (b) of Area C, both of which broke along the centerline. *a*, photo and drawing of a disc from square D15/c2. *b*, photo and drawing of a disc from square D15/d5.

Figure 10.6. The distribution of biconically drilled stone discs throughout the lower component (b) of Area C.

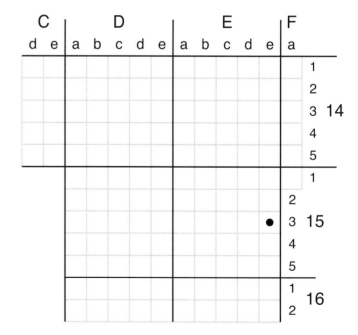

Figure 10.7. Photograph (*a*) and drawing (*b*) of a small biconically drilled stone disc from the upper component (a) of Area C. This disc, from square E15/e3, shows signs of an earlier drilling attempt that resulted in breakage (upper left side).

Figure 10.8. The location of the only biconically drilled stone disc recovered from the upper component (a) of Area C.

Part III

Ancillary Studies

Chapter 11

Pollen Samples

During the excavation of Gheo-Shih, project palynologist James Schoenwetter took three soil samples from the Jícaras phase deposits at the site. His hope was to recover enough pollen to cast light on the beginnings of agriculture in the Mitla region.

Two of his samples came from the Jícaras phase component of Area A; the third was taken from the lower component (b) of Area C.

Area A, square G29/c5[1]

A 78-grain pollen count from square G29/e5 of Area A yielded the following result:

Alnus: 1
Celtis-Moraceae: 1

1. Our counts for square G29/c5 correct a typographical error in Schoenwetter and Smith (2009: Table 15.28), where one grain of Celtis-Moraceae pollen was inadvertently omitted from the table. Schoenwetter himself caught this typo shortly after the publication of the Guilá Naquitz report and requested that we correct it when we published the Gheo-Shih site report.

Cheno-Am: 15
Hi Spine Compositae: 4
Lo Spine Compositae: 18
Graminae: 38
Zea sp.: 1

Area A, square G29/c2

A 100-grain pollen count from square G29/c2 yielded the following results:

Cheno-Am: 25
Lo Spine Compositae: 21
Graminae: 52
Leguminosae: 1
Quercus: 1

Area C, component b, square D15/d4

A 64-grain pollen count from square D15/d4 yielded the following results:

Alnus: 1
Cheno-Am: 3
Hi Spine Compositae: 2
Lo Spine Compositae: 10
Graminae: 45
Pinus: 1
Quercus: 1
Zea sp.: 1

Interpretation

Schoenwetter's untimely death prevented him from contributing a chapter to this volume. It therefore falls to us to interpret the results of his pollen identifications, drawing on his previous studies of Archaic samples from the Mitla region (Schoenwetter and Smith 2009).

Under today's environmental conditions, Gheo-Shih lies in what Kirkby et al. (2009) have called the grass facies of Mesquite Grassland B (see Chapter 1). The high frequencies of Graminae, or grass pollen, in Schoenwetter's samples could be considered consistent with Gheo-Shih's current grass facies setting. We are not convinced, however, that human land clearance in the Jícaras phase would have been as extensive as today's. Moreover, we note that Schoenwetter's samples include pollen grains from the legume family (Leguminosae) and the Celtis-Moraceae complex. This makes it likely that mesquite (*Prosopis* sp.)—a tree of the legume family—and the desert hackberry (*Celtis pallida*) were present near the site.

We therefore cannot rule out the possibility that during the Jícaras phase, Gheo-Shih lay in the órgano facies of Mesquite Grassland A, which even under today's conditions can be found only 100 meters from the site (see Figure 1.4). Kirkby et al. (2009:52) describe Mesquite Grassland A as "dominated by grass," and add that mesquite is "present though not abundant" in its órgano facies. As for the desert hackberry, whose fruit was eaten at Guilá Naquitz, it still grows near the Río Mitla, only 150 m from Gheo-Shih.

During the Jícaras phase, the Río Mitla would likely have been lined with alder and willow trees. We are therefore not surprised to find that Schoenwetter's samples produced two grains of alder pollen (*Alnus* sp.). Nor are we surprised by the grains of oak (*Quercus* sp.) and pine (*Pinus* sp.) pollen, since both trees would have been present in the "original" Mitla-area oak-pine forest reconstructed by C. E. Smith (1978). Even today, *Pinus michoacana* and *Quercus impressa* can be found in the mountains above Guilá Naquitz (Kirkby et al. 2009:49).

One of Schoenwetter's most exciting discoveries, to be sure, is the fact that two of his samples included grains of *Zea* pollen. What this suggests is that an early form of maize was being grown at Gheo-Shih during the Jícaras phase. This suggestion is reinforced by the discovery of five early maize cobs at Guilá Naquitz Cave (Figure 11.1). These cobs have been directly AMS dated to the Jícaras phase (see Benz 2001; Piperno and Flannery 2001).

As for the Compositae and Chenopod-Amaranth pollen grains from Schoenwetter's samples, there are limits to what we can say without knowing the actual species involved. We do know, however, that all the pollen samples Schoenwetter took from Formative village sites in Oaxaca were characterized by high frequencies of Cheno-Am pollen. Schoenwetter (personal communication, 1973) eventually concluded that such high Cheno-Am frequencies were typical of the weedy, fallow agricultural land that surrounds farming villages.

Our assessment of Gheo-Shih's pollen evidence is that during the Jícaras phase, the site lay in some Archaic version of Mesquite Grassland, and that the occupants had cleared a certain amount of riverine alluvium for the growing of early maize. Because of the evidence from Guilá Naquitz, we presume that they also grew squash and gourds, although there is no pollen evidence from Gheo-Shih to confirm this. There is even an outside chance that they were growing a species of runner bean whose cultivation was discontinued when superior bean species became available (see discussion in Flannery and Hole 2019:10). Based on the evidence from Guilá Naquitz, we also assume that the occupants of Gheo-Shih collected wild plants such as acorns, mesquite pods, and hackberries during the seasons when they were available.

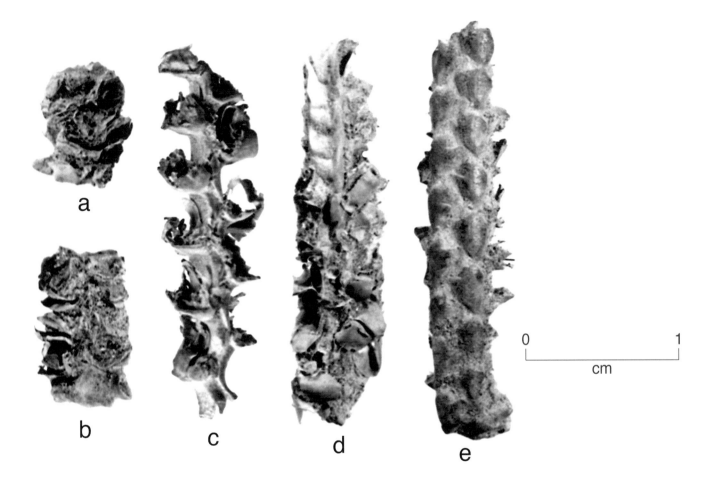

Figure 11.1. Five primitive maize cobs (or fragments thereof) found in ash lenses above Zone B1 at Guilá Naquitz. *a* and *b* are from Square C9; *c* is from Square D10; *d* and *e* are from Square D7. These cobs, shown here larger than life size, have been AMS dated to between 4355 and 4065 BC (calibrated).

Chapter 12

Radiocarbon Dates

Trying to get useful radiocarbon dates from Gheo-Shih was a frustrating experience. Even the occasional hearths we found did not have charcoal fragments sufficiently large for the radiocarbon requirements of the 1960s; their floors were reddened and blackened, but useful ash and carbon were hard to come by. We also did not trust charcoal from any level that could have been reached by a plow.

Fortunately, when Hole reached Feature 1—the stone-lined ritual feature lying on indurated Pleistocene alluvium at the bottom of Area A—he was lucky enough to find an in situ patch of charcoal large enough for two samples. Flannery sent half of that charcoal to Beta Analytic and received the following date:

Beta 190316: 8600 ± 40 BP
BP date minus 1950: 6650 BC
Dendrocalibrated 2-sigma range: 7630–7570 BC

Encouraged by these results, Flannery sent the other half of the sample to Beta Analytic and received a virtually identical date:

Beta 191398: 8600 ± 50 BP
BP date minus 1950: 6650 BC
Dendrocalibrated 2-sigma range: 7720–7560 BC

These dates indicate that our stone-lined ritual feature was constructed during the late Naquitz phase, and was therefore roughly contemporaneous with Zone B2 of Guilá Naquitz Cave (see Flannery 2009b: Table 1). In Chapter 13 we take advantage of this contemporaneity to compare a microband camp and a macroband camp of the Mitla Archaic.

Unfortunately, we were unable to recover a comparable charcoal sample from the overlying Jícaras phase levels at Gheo-Shih. The projectile points from Areas A and C leave no doubt about the Middle Archaic date of those levels, but it would have been nice to have absolute dates as well.

Fortunately, we have two Jícaras phase AMS dates on early maize cobs from Guilá Naquitz (Piperno and Flannery 2001). Those cobs had been recovered from small ash lenses at the cave, stratigraphically above Zone B1 and below the scatters of Formative potsherds that had been left in the cave before the Monte Albán IIIb–IV occupation of Zone A.

The early Guilá Naquitz maize cobs yielded the following dates:

Cob from Square D10
Beta 132510: 5410 ± 40 BP
BP date minus 1950: 3460 BC
Dendrocalibrated 2-sigma range: 4340–4220 BC

Cob from Square C9
Beta 132511: 5420 ± 60 BP
BP date minus 1950: 3470 BC
Dendrocalibrated 2-sigma range: 4355–4065 BC

We consider these dates relevant to the Jícaras phase occupation of Gheo-Shih, and would not be surprised to learn that the maize found at Guilá Naquitz was grown on the alluvium of the Río Mitla during the summer rainy season.

A Timeline for the Beginnings of Agriculture in Oaxaca

Our earliest evidence for agriculture in Oaxaca includes a pair of bottle gourd rinds from Zones C and B2 of Guilá Naquitz Cave. These gourd rinds produced calibrated AMS dates with two-sigma ranges of 8030–7915 BC and 7020–6595 BC, respectively. Our oldest *Cucurbita pepo* seed, from Zone C, produced a calibrated AMS date with a two-sigma range of 8035–7920 BC (B. D. Smith 1997). Clearly, therefore, the cultivation of cucurbits was well established during the Naquitz phase.

Some 161 pod valves of a runner bean (*Phaseolus* sp.) were present in Zone E of Guilá Naquitz, the oldest stratigraphic level. Kaplan (2009) designated these runner beans "Guilá Naquitz Type 1," but could not identify them to species because too many of the diagnostic parts were missing. These beans diminished in frequency during Zones D, C, and B1–B3, and apparently have since disappeared from the Mitla region. We cannot determine whether these runner beans were cultivated or collected in the wild, but we suspect that they were eventually abandoned in favor of superior domestic varieties.

As for maize, plant geneticists have determined that its ancestor is a subspecies of teosinte called *Zea mays* ssp. *parviglumis*, a wild grass native to the Balsas River drainage of Michoacán and Guerrero (Matsuoka et al. 2002). Piperno et al. (2009) have identified what they believe to be *Zea* phytoliths and starch grains from a rockshelter near Iguala, Guerrero, in what is today the heart of *parviglumis* territory. Wood charcoal from the same level as the phytoliths and starch grains has produced a radiocarbon date with a calibrated two-sigma range of 7040–6660 BC.

Ironically, circumstantial evidence for maize in the Mitla region is virtually as early. Schoenwetter and Smith (2009) identified *Zea* pollen from Zone B2 of Guilá Naquitz Cave, a level with a gourd rind whose calibrated AMS date has a two-sigma range of 7020–6595 BC. It is still the case, however, that our oldest actual maize cobs date to the fifth millennium BC, thousands of years later than the circumstantial pollen and phytolith evidence.

Taking all the currently available evidence into account, we feel confident in saying that the occupants of Gheo-Shih would have been cultivating maize with two-rowed cobs, *pepo* squash, and bottle gourds. A great deal of their diet, however, would have been provided by wild plants such as acorns, mesquite beans, agaves, prickly pear, and hackberries. The 50 projectile points from the site also make it clear that they were hunting deer and peccary with atlatls.

Part IV

Summary and Conclusions

Chapter 13

Gheo-Shih vs. Guilá Naquitz: The Differences between Microband and Macroband Camps

The fact that Gheo-Shih and Guilá Naquitz lie only 2.5 km apart presents us with a unique opportunity: we can now compare a microband camp and a macroband camp that are within walking distance of each other.

Aiding us in our comparison is the fact that we have radiocarbon dates from both sites. The basal level of Area A at Gheo-Shih has produced two dates with a dendrocalibrated two-sigma range of 7720–7560 BC. We can therefore look at the 35 Naquitz phase radiocarbon dates available from Guilá Naquitz Cave (Flannery 2009b: Table 1) to see which most closely matches the dates from Gheo-Shih. Date SI–515 from Zone B2, with a dendrocalibrated two-sigma range of 7995–7325 BC, comes the closest.

What this date suggests is that Feature 1 of Gheo-Shih and Zone B2 of Guilá Naquitz Cave were broadly contemporaneous. Both dated to the late Naquitz phase and could, potentially, be attributed to some of the same foragers. To be sure, we cannot prove that the same families moved between those two sites, but the fact that it is hypothetically possible justifies comparing them.

Let us begin with some obvious differences. Guilá Naquitz was a small cave—only 64 m²—and we doubt that it was occupied by more than 4–6 people. Gheo-Shih covered almost 1.5 ha, making it more than 200 times the area occupied by Guilá Naquitz. Even if we grant that Gheo-Shih may be a palimpsest of multiple superimposed camps, it is possible that it was at times occupied by 25–50 people. In order to reach that population level, some five to ten families the size of the one occupying Guilá Naquitz would have to have converged on Gheo-Shih.

We come now to the seasons during which these sites would have been occupied. At this point, the difference in plant preservation between a dry cave and an open-air site comes into focus. We know that Guilá Naquitz was occupied in the fall because of the 418 acorns and 12 *susí* nuts left behind on the Zone B2 living floor (Flannery 2009c: Table 24.17). Both of these nuts are products of the thorn forest zone in which Guilá Naquitz is located.

It is also the case, however, that 1613 mesquite seeds and 107 hackberry seeds were left behind on the Zone B2 living floor. What that means is that the foragers living in Guilá Naquitz Cave occasionally made a 2.5 km trip to the mesquite grassland zone to collect mesquite pods and hackberry fruits. A density contour map of the mesquite seeds left behind on the Zone B2 living floor suggests that this trip might have been made only once, resulting in one large pile of seeds in the northwest corner of the cave (Spencer and Flannery 2009: Figure 26.35). This is an area of the cave that often appeared to be a woman's work area (Reynolds 2009: Figure 28.31).

Here is where the complete absence of plant remains from Gheo-Shih presents a problem. We have suggested that Gheo-Shih might have been occupied during the summer rainy season, since this is when maize and *pepo* squash would most likely have been planted on the alluvium of the Río Mitla; it is also the peak season for harvesting the wild resources of the mesquite grassland zone, such as mesquite, hackberry, prickly pear, and acacia pods. While our suggestion is reasonable—and supported by the presence of maize pollen—it cannot be verified by actual macrobotanical plant remains.

Agave Roasting

Some 45 quids of chewed agave fiber were recovered from Zone B2 of Guilá Naquitz Cave (C. E. Smith 2009: Table 19.1). This makes it clear that one of the subsistence activities of the microband living there was to roast agave hearts. If one roasts the heart of *Agave potatorum*, one of the local species of agave, in an earth oven for 24–72 hours, it is rendered edible (Flannery 2009a:91). This process results in a considerable amount of firecracked rock. It is for this reason that we suspect that the hearths or roasting pits from the upper component (a) of Area C at Gheo-Shih might have been used for agave roasting. This, therefore, may constitute a shared activity between microband and macroband camps.

Ritual Activity

The basal level of Gheo-Shih's Area A produced Feature 1, a 20 m by 7 m cleared area presumed to be for ritual activity. Guilá Naquitz, on the other hand, produced no evidence for ritual activity at all. What this could mean is that late Naquitz phase foragers saved certain communal rituals for those moments when 25–50 people were living together at a macroband camp. This is a pattern documented for Native Americans of the western United States (see Chapter 4).

Ornament Making

Two areas of Gheo-Shih produced evidence of ornament making. In the Jícaras phase component of Area A, it involved oval stone pendants; in the lower component (b) of Area C, it involved biconically drilled stone discs. We suspect that the drilling of the stone discs (and perhaps the pendants as well) was carried out with large, hafted chert drills. In contrast, no evidence of ornament making whatsoever was found at Guilá Naquitz. What this may mean is that ornament manufacture tended to be carried out in macroband camps, when multiple families were living together. The fact that biconically drilled stone discs were found only in Area C suggests that some ornaments were made only by certain families or groups of residents, not by the entire population of a macroband camp.

A Comparison of Chipped Stone Tools

In addition to the similarities and differences already noted, we are of course curious to see how the two sites' chipped stone tool assemblages compare. Almost immediately we face a problem; if debitage is excluded, Zone B2 of Guilá Naquitz produced only 10 pieces of chipped stone, which seems too small a sample for any comparison. It is likely that for a meaningful comparison, we will have to compare the entire Archaic chipped stone assemblage from Guilá Naquitz with its equivalent at Gheo-Shih. To be sure, this means comparing a Naquitz phase assemblage to a Jícaras phase assemblage, but this should not be an insurmountable problem, since the main contrast in stone tools between the two phases is the stylistic difference in projectile points.

Table 13.1 compares 17 categories of chipped stone found at both Gheo-Shih (Areas A and C) and Guilá Naquitz (Zones E–B1); in each case, the raw tool count is followed by the percentage that each item contributes to the total from that site.

Our first impression is that the percentages are surprisingly similar; at both Gheo-Shih and Guilá Naquitz, the four most common categories are core fragments, notched flakes, utilized flakes, and steep denticulate scrapers.

To be sure, core fragments were 26% of the total at Gheo-Shih vs. 13% at Guilá Naquitz. It is not clear, however, how significant this difference is. Core fragments are not artifacts, but the result of destructive accidents; they are the kinds of items that might get thrown into what Binford (1978) called a "toss zone." Since Guilá Naquitz Cave measures only about 8 x 8 m, a core fragment tossed 5 m away might actually sail out the mouth of the cave and be lost on the talus slope. In Area A of Gheo-Shih, on the other hand, a core fragment tossed 5 m away would likely remain in the area we excavated. We will therefore not make too much of the difference in core fragment frequency between Gheo-Shih and Guilá Naquitz.

As we look at Table 13.1, one more point occurs to us: both sites have essentially the same tool inventory. In other words, even a family group no larger than 4–6 persons possessed the technical skills to make virtually all the tool types known from the Naquitz and Jícaras phases. While it may be the case that only certain families at macroband camps were engaged in ornament manufacture, every Archaic family seems to have been capable of making every category of chipped stone tool.

The Question of Men's and Women's Tools

We have names for the 17 most common types of Archaic chipped stone tools. Now we are curious to know which tools were used by men, which by women, and which by either or both.

At Guilá Naquitz, Flannery (2009c:431–432) made some tentative suggestions about the users of certain tools. Such suggestions were possible because plant and animal remains were abundant at Guilá Naquitz, and because Reynolds (2009) had used them to define activity areas and pathways for four of the cave's living floors, based on a multidimensional scaling program. A few of Flannery's (2009c) observations were as follows:

Hammerstones, core fragments, and debitage could occur in either men's or women's work areas, suggesting that primary chert knapping was likely done by both males and females.

Five out of seven steep denticulate scrapers had been discarded in pathways or work areas used mainly by women.

Three out of four burins had been discarded in pathways or work areas used mainly by women.

Twice as many notched flakes had been discarded in pathways or work areas used mainly by women as on pathways or work areas used mainly by men.

During our analysis of Cueva Blanca (Flannery and Hole 2019), Reynolds (2019) tried a different approach to distinguishing men's and women's tools. He stipulated, for the sake of argument, that projectile points were men's tools and flakes with sheen were women's tools. He then used rank-order correlation and cluster analysis to determine

Table 13.1. A comparison of tool frequencies at Gheo-Shih and Guilá Naquitz.

Tools	Gheo-Shih	Guilá Naquitz
Hammerstones	56 (.05)	8 (.05)
Flake cores	115 (.11)	11 (.07)
Core fragments	276 (.26)	19 (.13)
Utilized flakes	90 (.08)	21 (.14)
Notched flakes	200 (.19)	40 (.27)
Crude blades	47 (.04)	10 (.07)
Flakes with sheen	6 (.01)	6 (.04)
Choppers	--- (.00)	2 (.01)
End scrapers	15 (.01)	1 (.01)
Sidescrapers/knives	33 (.03)	4 (.03)
Steep denticulate scrapers	141 (.13)	13 (.09)
Burins	35 (.03)	4 (.03)
Drills	13 (.01)	1 (.01)
Bifaces, Variety A	3 (<.01)	-- (.00)
Bifaces, Variety B	14 (.01)	1 (.01)
Bifaces, Variety C	16 (.01)	5 (.03)
Projectile points	12 (.01)	4 (.03)
Debitage	18.441	1,564

which other tool types were positively or negatively associated with projectile points or flakes with sheen.

Rank correlation suggested that both Variety A bifaces and end scrapers were strongly associated with projectile points; on the other hand, projectile points were negatively associated with choppers, burins, and drills. Flakes with sheen were most strongly associated with crude blades (plain), discoidal cores, and core faces; on the other hand, they were negatively associated with bifaces of Varieties A and B, choppers, end scrapers, burins, and drills. (It is interesting that burins and drills, two "tools used to make other tools," stood apart from both hunting tools [projectile points] and plant-processing tools [flakes with sheen].)

Reynolds' cluster analysis yielded somewhat different results. In Zones E and D at Cueva Blanca, two living floors during whose occupation both men and women are believed to have been present, projectile points seemed to be part of a tool kit that included bifaces of Varieties A and B, end scrapers, and sidescrapers/knives. Flakes with sheen, on the other hand, were associated with crude blades (plain) and bifaces of Variety C. Once again, burins and drills seemed to be independent of either projectile points or flakes with sheen.

Armed with these suggestions from the analyses of Guilá Naquitz and Cueva Blanca, let us review some of the patterns we noticed in the Jícaras phase components at Gheo-Shih (see Chapter 6). In the Jícaras phase component of Area A, we detected an overlap between roughly semicircular alignments of hammerstones and flake cores. While this association may reflect the striking off of flakes from cores, the data from Guilá Naquitz suggest that both men and women engaged in that activity. For what it is worth, we also saw some evidence that 11–18 utilized flakes were also found with the hammerstone/flake core semicircles already mentioned. This suggests that some of the flakes struck off the cores may have been used for light cutting tasks not long after they were produced.

A second observation from the Jícaras phase component of Area A was that end scrapers and sidescrapers/knives were not discarded together, suggesting that they were used for different tasks. Perhaps our most interesting observation about this component is that burins and drills sometimes appeared to have been discarded together. This fact is interesting in light of Reynolds' (2019) conclusion that those two tool types were independent of both projectile points and flakes with sheen.

The lower component (b) of Area C provided us with our best evidence for ornament manufacture: four biconically drilled stone discs (Chapter 10). This evidence is enhanced by the presence, in that same component, of four chert drills that could have been used to carry out the biconical drilling. At least one of these drills was unusually large and had a stem by means of which it could have been hafted (Figure 5.63). To be sure, that still does not tell us whether these ornaments were made by men or women.

Let us now look at other potentially significant tool distributions from component b of Area C. Included are several tentative clusters of utilized flakes, two of which fall in areas where there are also numerous flake cores. This is a second case where circumstantial evidence suggests that some flakes may have been used for light cutting tasks not long after they were struck off.

There were also hints of an area where both crude blades (plain) and end scrapers were discarded together. We have no idea what kind of activity was involved; we can say, however, that sidescrapers/knives were apparently not discarded with end scrapers.

Finally, the burins from component b showed slight clustering, but in this case did not seem to have been discarded with drills.

The upper component (a) of Area C did not produce evidence of ornament manufacture comparable to that from component b; in fact, only two drills were recovered from component a.

The distribution of flake cores in component a was relatively dispersed; all potential clusters were small enough to suggest a series of individuals, each doing his or her flaking.

Perhaps the only tools whose distribution suggested one large work area were burins, seven of which had been discarded in the southern part of the excavation.

Conclusions

A comparison of Guilá Naquitz and Gheo-Shih suggests that even a microband of 4–6 individuals was capable of producing virtually all the chipped stone tool types seen at a macroband camp of 25–50 persons. The most striking difference in tools between the two types of sites was in ornament manufacture; Gheo-Shih produced biconically drilled stone discs and oval pendants, while Guilá Naquitz did not. Perhaps significantly, such ornament manufacture seems to have been localized at Gheo-Shih, suggesting that only certain families or residential groups carried it out. Finally, we found an area set aside for communal ritual activity at Gheo-Shih that is not matched by any feature at Guilá Naquitz. This suggests that certain rituals were performed only at those times of the year when the largest number of individuals were living together in a macroband camp.

Chapter 14

Gheo-Shih's Place in the Oaxaca Archaic

We will end this volume by considering Gheo-Shih's contribution to our understanding of the Archaic period in Oaxaca. Obviously we are pleased that Gheo-Shih provided our largest sample of Archaic chipped stone tools; we are disappointed, however, that no plant remains or animal bones were preserved at the site. Most importantly, we learned from Gheo-Shih that Oaxaca's Archaic foragers seem to have saved certain kinds of communal ritual and craft activity for those times when the largest number of families were encamped together.

The Archaic Sequence

We can interdigitate all the excavated components of our Archaic sequence as follows. The story begins with Zone F of Cueva Blanca (Flannery and Hole 2019), a level with Late Pleistocene fauna, including species no longer present in southern Mexico today. The Paleoindian–Archaic transition, based on radiocarbon dates from Feature 15 of Cueva Blanca, took place between (cal.) 11,810 BC and (cal.) 9870 BC.

The oldest living floor of the Early Archaic Naquitz phase—Zone E of Cueva Blanca—dates to somewhere between (cal.) 10,718 BC and 8304 BC. At this point, the Naquitz phase sequence picks up at Guilá Naquitz Cave (Flannery 2009b: Table 1). The 35 Naquitz phase radiocarbon dates from Guilá Naquitz make this our most extensively dated stage of the Archaic. These dates run from (cal.) 9005–8565 BC (Zone D) to (cal.) 6195–5980 BC (Zone B1). Combined with the dates from Cueva Blanca, they suggest that the Naquitz phase spanned the period from 10,000 BC to 6000 BC. During the second half of the Naquitz phase—(cal.) 7720–7560 BC—the macroband living at Gheo-Shih built a ritual feature consisting of a cleared area bounded by two parallel lines of boulders.

A number of significant processes took place during the Naquitz phase. Oaxaca's pinyon pines, which evidently had flourished under Pleistocene climatic conditions, gradually declined in number and disappeared by the end of the Naquitz phase. Domestic bottle gourds and *pepo* squash appeared in Oaxaca by (cal.) 8030–7915 BC. The Naquitz phase foragers were also harvesting hundreds of runner beans of what Kaplan (2009) calls "Guilá Naquitz *Phaseolus* Type 1"; unfortunately, Kaplan was unable to determine the species of these beans. Finally, Schoenwetter and Smith

(2009: Table 15.26) report grains of maize pollen from Zones B1 and B2 of Guilá Naquitz, suggesting that this important domesticate may have reached the Mitla region by (cal.) 7020–6595 BC. Unfortunately, we have no macrobotanical remains of maize from the Naquitz phase to confirm this.

The Naquitz phase does not align perfectly with any of MacNeish's Archaic phases from the Tehuacán Valley (Flannery 2009a: Table 3.1). The early Naquitz phase overlaps with MacNeish's Late Ajuereado phase, and those two phases share Lerma points (Hole 2009: Figures 6.26, 6.27). The late Naquitz phase partially overlaps with MacNeish's El Riego phase, and those two phases share Almagre points (Hole 2009: Figures 6.27, 6.28). Zone B3 of Guilá Naquitz, a late Naquitz living floor, produced our earliest example of the Pedernales point, a type that went on to reach peak popularity in the subsequent Jícaras phase (Hole 2009: Figures 6.29, 6.31).

A second Pedernales point, found on the surface near Guilá Naquitz, cannot be assigned to a phase; since we know that Guilá Naquitz was visited during the Jícaras phase, this second point could in fact be Middle Archaic.

Most of what we know about the Jícaras phase (6000–4000 BC) can be attributed to Gheo-Shih. We have concluded that during the summer rainy season, 25–50 Middle Archaic foragers-farmers camped in the mesquite grassland near the Río Mitla, supporting themselves by growing a variety of early domestic plants while harvesting mesquite pods and hackberry fruits. Five of the two-rowed maize cobs grown during this phase were discarded in ash lenses at Guilá Naquitz Cave at (cal.) 4355–4065 BC.

Area C of Gheo-Shih produced evidence for the manufacture of biconically drilled stone ornaments; Area A produced evidence for the manufacture of oval stone pendants. None of our Archaic caves or rockshelters provided comparable data for the creation of ornaments. We have concluded that ornament making was an activity carried out mainly at macroband camps. The evidence from Gheo-Shih also indicates that only certain areas of the site produced evidence for ornament making, suggesting that it may have been an activity limited to certain groups of residents. This is our first hint of the "family" or "neighborhood" craft specialization seen later in Formative villages like San José Mogote (Flannery and Marcus 2005).

Our excavations at Gheo-Shih make it clear how important the Pedernales point was as a diagnostic artifact for the Jícaras phase. Of the classifiable atlatl points from Gheo-Shih, 23 of 30 belonged to the Pedernales type. In none of our other Archaic phases was one point type this dominant. Not a single Pedernales point was recovered from Late Archaic Blanca phase levels at Cueva Blanca (Flannery and Hole 2019). It would seem that—at least in the Mitla region—this point type first appeared at the very end of the Naquitz phase, peaked in Jícaras times, and vanished at the start of the Blanca phase.

The Late Archaic Blanca phase is believed to have spanned the period from (cal.) 4000 BC to (cal.) 2300 BC; it is best known from Feature 18, Zone D, and Zone C at the site of Cueva Blanca (Flannery and Hole 2019:199–200). In terms of diagnostic artifacts, the Blanca phase saw an explosion in the diversity of its projectile point types. Among the types found in this phase were La Mina, Trinidad, Tilapa, San Nicolás, and Coxcatlán.

The presence of Coxcatlán points—made on nonlocal material—is particularly significant, since it suggests possible contacts with the Abejas phase foragers-farmers of the Tehuacán Valley (MacNeish et al. 1967:65). We also recovered Palmillas, Hidalgo, Abasolo, and Gary points from Blanca phase deposits, but for a variety of reasons these point types were less useful for establishing chronologies. Several of them had a long, multiperiod history in the Mitla region, and some too often seemed to be reworked or rejuvenated versions of other point types.

We are struck by the variety of point types in the Late Archaic, which might reflect either (1) increased social contact and the borrowing of ideas from neighboring groups, or (2) an effort by individual hunters to give the points they made a distinctive look, one that was recognizably theirs. The traditional !Kung San hunters of the Kalahari region were known to have done something similar with their arrows (Wiessner 1977).

As we explained in our report on Cueva Blanca (Flannery and Hole 2019), Zone C of the cave appears to represent a short-term camp made by a group of male hunters who killed at least two deer. We presume that these hunters came from, and later returned to, a Blanca phase macroband camp not unlike Gheo-Shih. What this suggests is that the Blanca phase witnessed what Binford (1980) has referred to as "logistically based collecting."

Our sample of Archaic sites is too small to document the exact moment at which the occupants of the Mitla region made the transition from "foraging" to "collecting" in Binford's terms. All we can suggest is that the transition was evident during the Blanca phase.

Sometime in the neighborhood of (cal.) 2500–2300 BC, the Blanca phase ended and the Martínez phase began. This phase, which we have previously characterized as the "last gasp" of the Archaic, is known only from the uppermost part of Stratigraphic Zone B of the Martínez Rockshelter (Flannery and Spores 2003:25). While this rockshelter was rich in prehistoric pollen (Schoenwetter and Smith

2009: Figure 15.5), it had no preservation of Archaic plant macrofossils or animal bones; as a result, Flannery excavated only about 17 m² of the site.

Stratigraphic Zone B produced Variety A bifaces, flake cores, steep denticulate scrapers, end scrapers, sidescrapers/knives, flakes with sheen, manos, metates, and mortars, but only a few pieces of atlatl points. In the uppermost part of this zone, Flannery found fragments of stone bowls like those recovered by MacNeish et al. (1967:117) from Late Archaic levels in the Tehuacán Valley.

> MacNeish felt that these stone bowls—some of which appeared to have been used for heating food—showed the need for a fire-resistant cooking vessel prior to the creation of pottery. An alternative possibility, of course, is that some of these labor-intensive vessels were used for consuming ritual beverages, such as pulque or chocolate. Here is a case where future residue analysis may provide answers. (Flannery and Hole 2019:201)

One of the least well-documented moments in Mexican prehistory is the transition from the Archaic to the Early Formative period. In the Valley of Oaxaca, that moment involved a decrease in projectile points in both number and variety; an increase in the number and variety of ground stone tools; and the initial appearance of pottery.

Gheo-Shih's Wider Significance

Finally, let us turn to Gheo-Shih's wider significance in the Archaic of the Mexican highlands. This volume is, to the best of our knowledge, only the second monograph-length report on a large open-air Archaic site from highland Mexico. The first was Christine Niederberger's monograph on her excavations at Zohapilco, a lacustrine macroband camp near Tlapacoya in the Basin of Mexico (Niederberger 1976).

Because the Archaic levels at Zohapilco lie buried beneath later (Formative) deposits, it is impossible to estimate the size of the Archaic campsite. The earliest occupation of Zohapilco took place during the Middle Archaic Playa phase, for which there are "sidereal dates" (an early version of calibration) of 5900 BC and 5115 BC. It is this phase that overlaps in time with Gheo-Shih.

The Playa phase occupants of Zohapilco lived on the shore of Lake Chalco-Xochimilco in the southern part of the Basin of Mexico. At that time, the lake would have been rich in small fish species (*Chirostoma* sp., *Girardinichthys* sp., and members of the Cyprinid family) and waterfowl (ducks, geese, grebes, and coots). Deer and rabbits would have been available on the floor and hills of the basin nearby. In addition, Niederberger recovered carbonized remains and/or pollen of husk tomatoes (*Physalis* sp.), squash (*Cucurbita* sp.), chenopods and amaranths, and *Zea* sp. (including a seed of the Chalco race of teosinte). This raises the possibility that the Playa phase residents of Zohapilco were cultivating early versions of these crop plants on the humid lakeshore soils (Niederberger 1979).

Unfortunately, it is difficult to compare the Playa phase stone tools to those of Gheo-Shih because of the difference in raw material. Gheo-Shih had ready access to silicified tuff and lay within walking distance of high-quality chert and chalcedony sources. Occupants of Zohapilco had ready access only to volcanic andesite, described by Niederberger (1979:135) as "difficult to work." The result is that many Playa phase tools are so crude as to be described by Niederberger (1979) as virtually "Clactonian."

Fortunately there was an obsidian source at Otumba, in the northeastern Basin of Mexico, which the occupants of Zohapilco could use for more delicate tools such as blades and projectile points. The latter are described by Niederberger (1979) as "stemmed with a convex base."

As far as we can tell, Zohapilco shared hammerstones, large bifaces, crude blades, utilized flakes, notched flakes, and scrapers of various kinds with Gheo-Shih. Included among the ground stone tools were one-hand manos, slab metates, basin-shaped metates, and mortars, usually made of andesite, basalt, or volcanic tuff.

Because the Playa phase levels at Zohapilco included animal species from both the winter dry season and the summer rainy season, Niederberger suggested that this lakeshore site might have been occupied year-round. While our minds are open on this subject, we would point to the fact that she recovered no evidence of permanent structures, and the area she excavated was apparently abandoned for 1500 years, beginning around 4500 BC (Niederberger 1979: Fig. 9). One of the thorniest problems in Archaic archaeology lies in determining whether a site was occupied year-round or simply occupied and reoccupied multiple times during the course of a year.

While we are pleased to see both Zohapilco and Gheo-Shih published in book-length format, we want more. Without question, there are other Archaic open-air macroband camps in the Mexican highlands that could be excavated and published; we need a sample large enough so that we understand the range of variation. Both Scotty MacNeish and Christine Niederberger saw open-air macroband camps as the ancestors of the Early Formative village, a scenario that can only be confirmed by excavating an adequate sample of open-air Archaic sites.

Appendix A

Resumen en Español

by Jhon Cruz Quiñones

Gheo-Shih es un campamento de 1.5 hectáreas perteneciente al periodo Arcaico Medio, localizado a 4 kilómetros al oeste de Mitla, Oaxaca, México. El sitio se encuentra a una altitud de 1660 metros sobre el nivel del mar, en una ladera ligeramente inclinada con vistas hacia la planicie aluvial del Río Mitla. Este río se ubica a sólo 150 metros del sitio.

De acuerdo con la terminología del arqueólogo Richard S. MacNeish, Gheo-Shih fue un "campamento de macro-bandas", concepto que indica una población estimada de entre 25 y 50 personas. En el modelo de caza-recolección y agricultura incipiente propuesto por MacNeish para la sierra sur de México, los cazadores-recolectores pasaban parte del año dispersos en pequeños grupos de "micro-bandas" compuestos por 4–6 individuos. Únicamente cuando los recursos eran abundantes en una localidad específica, tales grupos familiares de bandas dispersas se unían para conformar campamentos grandes como el de Gheo-Shih. Por esta razón, Gheo-Shih ha dado a Frank Hole y Kent Flannery la oportunidad de comparar las actividades de un campamento de macro-bandas con la cueva de Guilá Naquitz, un campamento de micro-bandas de 64 m² ubicado a sólo 2.5 kilómetros de distancia.

La primera fase de la investigación en Gheo-Shih fue un reconocimiento completo de la superficie usando una retícula de 5 m². A continuación, cada uno de los cuadrantes fue dividido en 25 unidades de 1 x 1m que permitió la excavación del sitio en unidades de 1 m².

Las profundidades de los depósitos de Gheo-Shih fueron examinadas a cada 5 metros usando esbeltas sondas de metal para muestreo de suelos; posteriormente las áreas de mayor profundidad fueron examinadas con pozos de sondeo de 1 x 1 m. Basado en los resultados de los pozos de sondeo, dos grandes áreas fueron excavadas hasta la capa estéril, la cual era extremadamente dura resultado de un aluvión del Pleistoceno.

Las dos áreas enteramente excavadas fueron el Área A (451 m²) y el Área C (136 m²). El Área A tuvo dos niveles estratigráficos. El nivel inferior, datado para el momento tardío de la fase Naquitz, arrojó dos fechados radiocarbónicos de 6650 a.C. (7720–7560 fechas calibradas a.C.). En este nivel se halló el Elemento 1, un rasgo ritual de 7 m de ancho cercado entre dos líneas paralelas de rocas dispuestas a lo largo de 20 m. El Elemento 1 se asemeja a un "campo de baile" similar a los creados por los cazadores recolectores de California y Nevada en el oeste de los Estados Unidos.

El nivel superior del Área A perteneció a la fase Jícaras (6000–4000 a.C.). Este nivel produjo 581 artefactos de pedernal, incluyendo tres puntas de dardo para *átlatl* del tipo Pedernales. Este tipo fue la punta de dardo para *átlatl* más común de la fase Jícaras; de las 30 puntas de Gheo-Shih que pudieron ser clasificadas, 23 fueron del tipo Pedernales. Lo que distingue al nivel superior del Área A son los ornamentos de piedra rosada.

El Área C no tuvo depósitos de la fase Naquitz. Por el contrario, tuvo dos niveles superpuestos de la fase Jícaras. El nivel inferior—"b"—produjo 340 artefactos de pedernal. Quizás los artefactos más distintivos del nivel inferior fueron una serie de ornamentos circulares de roca con un orificio central perforado con forma bicónica, aparentemente hechos con un gran perforador de pedernal.

El nivel superior del Área C—"a"—produjo 159 artefactos de pedernal. Este nivel también tenía una serie de hornos, posiblemente usados para la cocción de corazones de agave.

El Área C produjo 9 puntas de dardo para *átlatl* o fragmentos de puntas. Cuatro de ellas correspondían al tipo Pedernales; también se halló una punta Palmillas, una punta Hidalgo y una punta Abasolo.

Al comparar Gheo-Shih (un campamento de macro-bandas) con la cueva de Guilá Naquitz (un campamento de micro-bandas), se puede llegar a las siguientes conclusiones:

1. Aunque Guilá Naquitz fue ocupada por sólo 4–6 personas, produjo los 17 tipos de herramientas de pedernal hallados en Gheo-Shih en proporciones similares—por ejemplo núcleos, lascas utilizadas, raspadores de diversos tipos, buriles, perforadores, bifaciales ovoides, etcétera.
2. Mientras Gheo-Shih se caracterizó por el Elemento 1, un "campo de baile" ritual, Guilá Naquitz no tuvo ninguna evidencia de rituales. Este hecho sugiere que ciertos rituales fueron realizados únicamente en aquellas ocasiones en que 25–50 personas se congregaban para vivir juntos.
3. Mientras el Área C de Gheo-Shih manufacturaba ornamentos circulares de roca, aparentemente Guilá Naquitz no produjo ningún ornamento. Al parecer, la producción de ornamentos se realizó únicamente en los campamentos de macro-bandas y, para el caso de Gheo-Shih, sólo por algunas familias (en el Área C).

Para concluir, se recuperó polen de maíz en los niveles de la fase Jícaras en Gheo-Shih, sugiriendo que una de las actividades que se llevaron a cabo fue el cultivo de los suelos aluviales del Río Mitla. Esta área también es una zona donde las vainas del mesquite (*Prosopis* sp.) y los frutos del rompecapa (*Celtis* sp.) pueden ser recolectados durante la temporada de lluvias (de mayo a septiembre).

References

Benz, Bruce F.
    2001. Archaeological evidence of teosinte domestication from Guilá Naquitz, Oaxaca. *Proceedings of the National Academy of Sciences* 98:2104–2106.

Binford, Lewis R.
    1978. Dimensional analysis of behavior and site structure: Learning from an Eskimo hunting stand. *American Antiquity* 43(3):330–361.
    1980. Willow smoke and dogs' tails: Hunter-gatherer settlement systems and archaeological site formation. *American Antiquity* 45(1):4–20.

Binford, Lewis R., Sally R. Binford, Robert Whallon, and Margaret Ann Hardin
    1970. Archaeology at Hatchery West. *Memoirs of the Society for American Archaeology* No. 24. Washington, DC.

D'Azevedo, Warren Leonard (editor)
    1986. *Handbook of North American Indians, Vol. 11: Great Basin*. Washington, DC: Smithsonian Institution.

Flannery, Kent V.
    2003. Settlement, subsistence, and social organization of the Proto-Otomangueans. In *The Cloud People: Divergent Evolution of the Zapotec and Mixtec Civilizations* (revised edition), edited by Kent V. Flannery and Joyce Marcus, pp. 32–36. Clinton Corners, NY: Percheron Press.
    2009a. *Guilá Naquitz: Archaic Foraging and Early Agriculture in Oaxaca, Mexico* (updated edition). Walnut Creek, CA: Left Coast Press.
    2009b. Foreword to the updated edition (2009a). In *Guilá Naquitz: Archaic Foraging and Early Agriculture in Oaxaca, Mexico* (updated edition), edited by Kent V. Flannery, pp. xix–xxii. Walnut Creek, CA: Left Coast Press.
    2009c. Episodal analysis of Guilá Naquitz: A synthesis of Spencer's, Whallon's, and Reynolds' results. In *Guilá Naquitz: Archaic Foraging and Early Agriculture in Oaxaca, Mexico* (updated edition), edited by Kent V. Flannery, pp. 425–432. Walnut Creek, CA: Left Coast Press.

Flannery, Kent V. and Frank Hole
    2019. *Cueva Blanca: Social Change in the Archaic of the Valley of Oaxaca*. Memoirs of the Museum of Anthropology, University of Michigan, No. 60. Ann Arbor.

Flannery, Kent V. and Joyce Marcus
- 2003a. The growth of site hierarchies in the Valley of Oaxaca: Part I. In *The Cloud People: Divergent Evolution of the Zapotec and Mixtec Civilizations* (revised edition), edited by Kent V. Flannery and Joyce Marcus, pp. 53–64. Clinton Corners, NY: Percheron Press.
- 2003b. Urban Mitla and its rural hinterland. In *The Cloud People: Divergent Evolution of the Zapotec and Mixtec Civilizations* (revised edition), edited by Kent V. Flannery and Joyce Marcus, pp. 295–300. Clinton Corners, NY: Percheron Press.
- 2005. *Excavations at San José Mogote 1: The Household Archaeology*. Memoirs of the Museum of Anthropology, University of Michigan, No. 40. Ann Arbor.
- 2015. *Excavations at San José Mogote 2: The Cognitive Archaeology*. Memoirs of the Museum of Anthropology, University of Michigan, No. 58. Ann Arbor.

Flannery, Kent V. and Ronald Spores
- 2003. Excavated sites of the Oaxaca preceramic. In *The Cloud People: Divergent Evolution of the Zapotec and Mixtec Civilizations* (revised edition), edited by Kent V. Flannery and Joyce Marcus, pp. 20–26. Clinton Corners, NY: Percheron Press.

Hole, Frank
- 2009. Chipped stone tools. In *Guilá Naquitz: Archaic Foraging and Early Agriculture in Oaxaca, Mexico* (updated edition), edited by Kent V. Flannery, pp. 97–139. Walnut Creek, CA: Left Coast Press.

Holmes, William Henry
- 1897. Archaeological studies among the ancient cities of Mexico (Part II): Monuments of Chiapas, Oaxaca and the Valley of Mexico. *Field Columbian Museum Anthropological Series* 1(1). Chicago.

Kaplan, Lawrence
- 2009. Preceramic *Phaseolus* from Guilá Naquitz. In *Guilá Naquitz: Archaic Foraging and Early Agriculture in Oaxaca, Mexico* (updated edition), edited by Kent V. Flannery, pp. 281–284. Walnut Creek, CA: Left Coast Press.

Kirkby, Michael J., Anne V. Whyte, and Kent V. Flannery
- 2009. The physical environment of the Guilá Naquitz Cave Group. In *Guilá Naquitz: Archaic Foraging and Early Agriculture in Oaxaca, Mexico* (updated edition), edited by Kent V. Flannery, pp. 43–61. Walnut Creek, CA: Left Coast Press.

Liljeblad, Sven and Catherine S. Fowler
- 1986. Owens Valley Paiute. In *Handbook of North American Indians, Vol. 11: Great Basin*, edited by Warren L. D'Azevedo, pp. 412–434. Washington, DC: Smithsonian Institution.

Lorenzo, José Luis
- 1958. Un sitio precerámico en Yanhuitlán, Oaxaca. *Instituto Nacional de Antropología e Historia, Dirección Prehistoria, Publicación* 6. México, D.F.

Lowie, Robert H.
- 1915. *Dances and Societies of the Plains Shoshone*. Anthropological Papers of the American Museum of Natural History, Vol. 11, pt. 10. New York.

MacNeish, Richard S.
- 1964. Ancient Mesoamerican civilization. *Science* 143:531–537.
- 1972. The evolution of community patterns in the Tehuacán Valley of Mexico and speculations about the cultural processes. In *Man, Settlement, and Urbanism*, edited by Peter J. Ucko, Ruth Tringham, and G. W. Dimbleby, pp. 67–93. London: Gerald Duckworth and Co.

MacNeish, Richard S., Antoinette Nelken-Terner, and Irmgard W. Johnson
- 1967. *The Prehistory of the Tehuacán Valley*, Volume 2: *Nonceramic Artifacts*. Austin: University of Texas Press.

Matsuoka, Yoshihiro, Yves Vigouroux, Major M. Goodman, Jesús Sánchez G., Edward Buckler, and John Doebley
- 2002. A single domestication for maize shown by multilocus microsatellite genotyping. *Proceedings of the National Academy of Sciences* 99:6080–6084.

Niederberger, Christine
- 1976. *Zohapilco: Cinco milenios de ocupación humana en un sitio lacustre de la cuenca de México*. Colección Científica 30. México, D.F.: Instituto Nacional de Antropología e Historia.
- 1979. Early sedentary economy in the Basin of Mexico. *Science* 203:131–142.

Parry, William
- 1987. *Chipped Stone Tools in Formative Oaxaca, Mexico: Their Procurement, Production and Use*. Memoirs of the Museum of Anthropology, University of Michigan, No. 20. Ann Arbor.

Piperno, Dolores R. and Kent V. Flannery
- 2001. The earliest archaeological maize (*Zea mays* L.) from highland Mexico: new accelerator mass spectrometry dates and their implications. *Proceedings of the National Academy of Sciences* 98:2101–2103.

Piperno, Dolores R., Anthony J. Ranere, Irene Holst, José Iriarte, and Ruth Dickau
- 2009. Starch grain and phytolith evidence for early ninth millennium B.P. maize from the central Balsas River Valley, Mexico. *Proceedings of the National Academy of Sciences* 106:5019–5024.

Reynolds, Robert G.
- 2009. Multidimensional scaling of four Guilá Naquitz living floors. In *Guilá Naquitz: Archaic Foraging and Early Agriculture in Oaxaca, Mexico* (updated edition), edited by Kent V. Flannery, pp. 385–423. Walnut Creek, CA: Left Coast Press.
- 2019. The search for tool kits at Cueva Blanca: Two statistical approaches. In *Cueva Blanca: Social Change in the Archaic of the Valley of Oaxaca*, by Kent V. Flannery and Frank Hole, pp. 168–183. Memoirs of the Museum of Anthropology, University of Michigan, No. 60. Ann Arbor.

Schoenwetter, James and Landon Douglas Smith
- 2009. Pollen analysis of the Oaxaca Archaic. In *Guilá Naquitz: Archaic Foraging and Early Agriculture in Oaxaca, Mexico* (updated edition), edited by Kent V. Flannery, pp. 179–237. Walnut Creek, CA: Left Coast Press.

Smith, Bruce D.
- 1997. The initial domestication of *Cucurbita pepo* in the Americas 10,000 years ago. *Science* 276:932–934.

Smith, C. Earle, Jr.
- 1978. *The Vegetational History of the Oaxaca Valley*. Memoirs of the Museum of Anthropology, University of Michigan, No. 10, Part I. Ann Arbor.
- 2009. Preceramic plant remains from Guilá Naquitz. In *Guilá Naquitz: Archaic Foraging and Early Agriculture in Oaxaca, Mexico* (updated edition), edited by Kent V. Flannery, pp. 265–274. Walnut Creek, CA: Left Coast Press.

Spencer, Charles S. and Kent V. Flannery
- 2009. Spatial variation of debris at Guilá Naquitz: a descriptive approach. In *Guilá Naquitz: Archaic Foraging and Early Agriculture in Oaxaca, Mexico* (updated edition), edited by Kent V. Flannery, pp. 331–367. Walnut Creek, CA: Left Coast Press.
- 2019. Distributional variability in Zones E–C of Cueva Blanca: a local analysis of grid-density data. In *Cueva Blanca: Social Change in the Archaic of the Valley of Oaxaca*, by Kent V. Flannery and Frank Hole, pp. 149–167. Memoirs of the Museum of Anthropology, University of Michigan, No. 60. Ann Arbor.

Steward, Julian
- 1938. *Basin-Plateau Aboriginal Sociopolitical Groups*. Bureau of American Ethnology Bulletin of the Smithsonian Institution 120. Washington, DC: Smithsonian Institution.
- 1955. *Theory of Culture Change*. Urbana, IL: University of Illinois Press.

Thomas, David Hurst, Lorann S. A. Pendleton, and Stephen C. Cappannari
- 1986. Western Shoshone. In *Handbook of North American Indians, Vol. 11: Great Basin*, edited by Warren L. D'Azevedo, pp. 262–283. Washington, DC: Smithsonian Institution.

Whalen, Michael E.
- 2009. Sources of the Guilá Naquitz chipped stone. In *Guilá Naquitz: Archaic Foraging and Early Agriculture in Oaxaca, Mexico* (updated edition), edited by Kent V. Flannery, pp. 141–146. Walnut Creek, CA: Left Coast Press.

Wiessner, Polly
- 1977. *Hxaro: A Regional System of Reciprocity for Reducing Risk Among the !Kung San*. PhD dissertation, Department of Anthropology, University of Michigan, University Microfilms, Ann Arbor.

Williams, Howel and Robert F. Heizer
- 1965. Geological notes on the ruins of Mitla and other Oaxacan sites, Mexico. *Contributions of the University of California Archaeological Research Facility* 1:41–54.